"*The Common Good* captures personalism's core insight, interpersonal relations as the key to understanding God, Persons, and the world. This presentation of personalism is the first, as far as I know, to present personalism to a general audience. From that perspective, *The Common Good*, accomplishes an important goal: Personalism is central to daily grappling with our common lives together. Pulled to something greater than ourselves, we must embrace personalism with unrelenting passion."

THOMAS O. BUFORD, professor, Furman University, North Carolina, USA

"I very much enjoyed reading *The Common Good*. The book does an excellent job of conveying what personalism is about that certainly will be understandable to a general reader, as well as of interest to personalist academics."

JAMES BEAUREGARD, Rivier University, Nashua, New Hampshire, USA

"Jonas Norgaard has done a great job by exposing the personalist thought brilliantly adapted to the mentality and interests of the 21st century. Combining his skills as a communicator with precision in presenting the authors, he has been able to present the main anthropological and social keys of personalism in a format close to all readers."

JUAN MANUEL BURGOS, professor, San Pablo University, Spain

"I found it a very enjoyable and interesting read – a grand piece of work that does the job of presenting what is, in many ways, quite a straightforward and pragmatic philosophy to a wider audience which definitely deserves to know much more about the subject.

By bringing this vital and exciting tradition to public attention, this book presents a crucial challenge to the philosophical, political, and cultural status quo. It does so, moreover, in a remarkably engaging and readable way. It may also prove to be a great contribution to the development of a popular public philosophical discourse."

SIMON SMITH, Independent Scholar, Haslemere, Surrey, UK

"In his book Norgaard Mortensen gives a convincing introduction to this current of thought, and takes a step forward in revealing it's importance in the public sector.

Prof. Mortensen's current work is an accurate and non-technical account of the main characteristics present in the life and work of many important authors that have put the human person in the forefront of their intellectual reflection and praxis."

JORGE OLAECHEA CATTER, director, Vida Y Espiritualiddad, Lima, Peru

"Jonas Norgaard Mortensen's work will undoubtedly satisfy the expectations of a number of readers who were left disappointed by specialist theses, available to a narrow range of experts. The publication is attractive because it can serve as a reference book, enabling people to acquaint themselves with the basic assumptions of the personalistic philosophy and its application in the creation of common good."

KRZYSZTOF GUZOWSKI, professor, John Paul II Catholic University of Lublin (KUL), Lublin, Poland

"This is a very good book and Jonas have done us all a great service in writing it."

RANDALL AUXIER, professor, Southern Illinois University, editor of the journal *The Personalist Forum* (renamed *The Pluralist* in 2005), USA

"I am both shocked and moved to find that personalism, the existence of which I was unaware of until now, seems to be the common thread that runs through all of my passionate commitments, present and past, as far back as I can remember. The book hits the exact spot where my heart beats, my tears flow, and my courage to work for change is rekindled."

KAREN LUMHOLT, journalist, author and director of think tank Cura, Denmark

"An extremely well-written introduction to personalism, a virtually unknown philosophical and political current that holds great inspiration for our way of building and leading communities. A break with an often stereotypical polarization of individual over against community, by looking at relationships as what connects each of us with others. In the family, the workplace, and in the world. Do we build up or do we tear down? We face this choice every day in our communication, behavior, and management."

Thomas Johansen, director, partner and head consultant
in the consultancy MacMann Berg

"How desperately we need the view of humans that permeates personalism and the book The Common Good. It is a holistic view of humans, it is about respect for values and social relations, and it is about the belief that we, in a community, can change the world and our own existence. Personalism is fundamentally about becoming responsible: our ability to take responsibility—and to share it.

The book dusts off an old theory and demonstrates its vast relevance in our current age and world. It does so by involving brand new knowledge about social relationships from surveys and theories in the human and social sciences. The book will therefore be of value to anyone working in the social sector."

Per Schultz-Jørgensen, Professor of Psychology,
Danish School of Education

"The notion that all humans are dignified, relational, and engaged is a subcurrent of my entire work with young people in boarding schools. In conversations, dialogue, and behavior, this view of humans comes to the surface and gives content and body to the claim that "All young people wish to succeed". The book The Common Good should be read by anybody working with children and young people."

Jan Dufke, Headmaster, Skovbo Boarding School

"In these times when the crisis of culture and management seems to have become permanent, it is wonderful to see a book that grapples with a challenging and inspirational new perspective. The book is a welcome and vitalizing unpacking of ideas that will resonate with the growing number of people who are all fighting for a new and better future. Read the book; it is an important and benevolent appeal for society to rise up and re-conquer our social institutions as human domains."

STIG SKOV MORTENSEN
Head of SOPHIA – think tank for pedagogics and social formation

"As I read the second edition of The Common Good, I was shocked to discover the pertinence and centrality of some of the book's points in light of recent developments in national and international society. We are witnessing a social shift in which community and dialogue become ever more trapped between political correctness and populist darkness. In this post-factual haze, The Common Good can help us navigate towards deeply founded values, frames, and relational points of orientation that provide air for our development and well-being to grow in."

KARSTEN AUERBACH, painter

"A growing number of people are becoming involved in volunteer efforts centered around relationships, because the way we interact defines the life we live and the society that we are part of. The Common Good articulates the importance of this fact and provides insight as well as new inspiration for a future with humans at the center."

JAKOB I. MYSCHETZKY, Development Manager, Danish Refugee Council / Frivillignet (Volunteer Department)

"Personalism has always helped me in my work in organization development, namely as an essential contribution to the balancing of the classical dilemmas always present in such work—for instance in finding the right balance between bureaucracy and emergent aspects, between control and freedom, and between uniformity and diversity."

Henrik Schelde Andersen, chief consultant, COK

"We live in an age when representative democracy is incapable of accommodating the true and good values of community in the struggle against dark forces.
The book The Common Good sets the direction for a new political culture that ascribes to each one of us social as well as political responsibility in order for us to contribute to the renewal of society. The language and magic of art may here be a crucial source of inspiration."

Preben Melander, professor, Centre for Business Development and Management, Copenhagen Business School

"The Common Good sets the direction for a new political culture that ascribes to each one of us social as well as political responsibility in order for us to contribute to the renewal of society."

Preben Melander, professor, Centre for Business Development and Management, Copenhagen Business School

Jonas Norgaard Mortensen

The Common Good

An Introduction to Personalism

Vernon Series in Philosophy

Copyright © 2017 Vernon Press, an imprint of Vernon Art and Science Inc, on behalf of the author.

All rights reserved. No part of this publication may be reproduced, stored in a retrieval system, or transmitted in any form or by any means, electronic, mechanical, photocopying, recording, or otherwise, without the prior permission of Vernon Art and Science Inc.

www.vernonpress.com

In the Americas:
Vernon Press
1000 N West Street,
Suite 1200, Wilmington,
Delaware 19801
United States

In the rest of the world:
Vernon Press
C/Sancti Espiritu 17,
Malaga, 29006
Spain

Vernon Series in Philosophy
Library of Congress Control Number: 2017934779
ISBN: 978-1-62273-234-0

Translation and adaptation from the original Danish version:
Benjamin Marco Dalton

Cover design by Vernon Press, using elements selected by freepik

Product and company names mentioned in this work are the trademarks of their respective owners. While every care has been taken in preparing this work, neither the authors nor Vernon Art and Science Inc. may be held responsible for any loss or damage caused or alleged to be caused directly or indirectly by the information contained in it.

Contents

Foreword by Thomas O. Buford	13
Introduction	17
The Relational Human **You and I, Alfred**	29
The Engaged Human **You Are Free for Community**	57
The Dignified Human **You Are One of a Kind**	81
Challenges to Personalism **You and I – on Our Way**	111
Postscript **Psychology and personalism**	129
Notes	153
Index	163
About the Author	168

Foreword

In *The Common Good* Jonas Norgaard Mortensen shows that personalism is contemporary, up-to-date, a living philosophy for people. It is not an esoteric, narrow activity practiced by a few intellectuals protected by the walls of academia. To make his point, Mortensen calls our attention to a current crisis that penetrates to the core of Western societies and shows that personalism offers a penetrating analysis, and a compelling vision for our societies, a direction we should walk to find meaning in our lives.

Consider the meaning of "crisis." It is a situation in which we cannot go back to what we have been doing; yet we do not know in what direction we should proceed. For example, the American Congress is stymied by unbending ideologies that lead economically to a situation in which the rich get richer and the poor get poorer. To what can we appeal to lead us beyond this malaise? Examine the crisis from the viewpoint of personalism.

Jonas lays bare personalism, its anthropology, and three core principles: humans are relational, they engage, and they have inherent dignity. Persons live best in close interpersonal relations with dignified humans. When examined through the lenses of personalism, we find the crisis has a structure, learn how those structures permeate our lives and the societies in which we live, and discover a way of overcoming the crisis.

In the Western World we live in a period of economic and political crisis, a crisis that affects every dimension of our society. How deep and pervasive is it? Since the economies of most of the Western World are capitalistic or influenced by capitalism, it is plausible that capitalism influences (possibly overlaying and controlling) all other institutions, from education, religion, politics, family, and communication, to law. This pervasive influence, however, raises questions not only about our institutions and their relationships but also about economic well-being itself.

While it is important to have a job that provides money to care for our families and ourselves, we wonder if economic power, jobs, and money provide the meaning we deeply seek. Our politicians work to create jobs and tell us to work hard. In doing so they point in one of two directions: individualism and individual responsibility or the group, collectivism, socialism, caring for the poor, the helpless, the sick. Both alternatives are economic solutions to our problems; they are also deeply ideological. Politicians claim that moving in the direction they propose will give us the way of life we all want. But does it? Is the life good to live found there or somewhere else?

In light of personalism's core principles, individualism and socialism are recognized as abstractions uprooted from their life giving soil. Instead of "us" and "we" together, inter-related, we treat ourselves as individuals or members of a group. Overemphasizing the importance of the individual, we objectify other people and find ourselves alienated from them and ourselves. Focusing on groups, we attempt to understand them through structures such as ideologies, systems, and institutions. Ignoring our interpersonal lives and looking to individualism or socialism, we find only depersonalization, narcissism, loneliness, alienation, systemic objectification, and mistrust.

In *The Common Good*, Mortensen focuses on the lives of persons-in-relation that enhance rather than depersonalize, that in twenty-first century points the way beyond the present crisis brought on by individualism and socialism to relations of mutual trust and understanding and to lives good to live.

Personalism has a long, honored history with roots in Athens, Rome, Jerusalem, and India. In placing before you the core principles of personalism, Jonas honors that history and cites important modern and contemporary personalists, from Martin Luther King, Jr., Mounier, Berdyaev, to Karol Wojtyla. They call us to a philosophy that focuses on our relationships with each other, where meaningful life is found.

The Common Good opens the windows of personalism to help us see a way of thinking that expands our imaginations to set us on the way to the good common to us all. In these pages, personalism comes alive.

>THOMAS O. BUFORD
>Louis G. Forgione Professor of Philosophy, Emeritus
>Furman University
>Greenville, South Carolina

Introduction

We live in what we in the Western World call a time of crisis. A period of economic progress has given way to pessimism and bewilderment. It seems to be broadly agreed that the economic crisis has taken hold and may last several years, and yet there are no clear guidelines as to how we might move on. Simultaneously, the consequences of global climate change have begun to show, especially in the Third World. As far as we can tell, this set of problems seems likely to remain the great challenge for world leaders throughout the present century.

Crises are not something purely negative, though they may be grave enough for those suffering the consequences. One good thing about crises is that they provide an opportunity for us to reconsider our priorities as to what is most important in life. To ponder what we might call the big questions: What is the purpose of our lives and how does one attain a good life? Upon which values should our societies be built, and in what direction are we as a community moving? In a word: What's the point of it all?

The interesting – and depressing – thing is that, with very few exceptions, these big questions are neither asked nor answered by politicians. In the political world, attention has been directed almost exclusively towards the economy, and for several years *growth* has been the mantra of nearly every political party. It is symptomatic that not even those most critical of capitalism have abandoned the concept of growth, speaking instead of "green growth" or the like.

This puts us in a grotesque situation where politicians greet us in near unison with the message that "citizens must work more hours" because this is what "the economic system" demands, a necessity for our "welfare." But at the same time, many of us have found by experience that more work – and more material wealth – does not make us more happy. Quite the contrary. High on the list of things that people regret on their deathbed is having spent too much time working.[1]

It does not take a very extensive or thorough analysis to establish that wealth does not guarantee happiness in life, not by a long shot. To be sure, this insight is by no means new. Wealth does not by necessity equal welfare. Regardless, we have managed to create societies defined to a great extent by economic thought, and it seems that human values have been forced into the background.

In a quiet moment, we might ask ourselves: Are there really no alternatives to working our way out of the crisis? Or to buying more flat screen TV sets? Is this ultimately what will bring about a better life for us? Or might we imagine an approach different from the one offered by the political left and right alike, with slight variation?

Individual or society

The European nation states can, to a varying degree, be seen as a number of attempts to combine the best of what is traditionally called the political "left" and "right" – care for the weak on the one hand and personal freedom on the other. The same may reasonably be said of the more liberal trends in American politics. The terms "left" and "right" usually stand for some variety of the ideological and historical heritage of *socialism* and *liberalism*, respectively.

This is not to say that the political left in general is associated with the totalitarian horrors of the 20th century state communism. The point is, rather, that socialism as an intellectual current may take, and indeed has taken, many other, more moderate forms. These forms of moderate socialism have mainly influenced the political left. Conversely, the intellectual heritage from Adam Smith and his economic liberalism is manifested mainly in the political right.

One internationally well-known variety of such left-right synthesis is the so-called "Scandinavian model" which attempts to mold a society in which all citizens share a part, and where "few people have too much, and still fewer have too little," as priest and popular educator N. F. S. Grundtvig put it.[2]

For many years the struggle between right and left – between individualism and collectivism – has been the natural point of orientation in any political debate. These have been the models that were ready at hand, and our political solutions have been informed by this opposition – in the sense that one is either in favor of more freedom or of more community. Take, for instance, the sentiment of Democrat liberals in the U.S. that the government should have enough power to actively care for its citizens subject to it, as opposed to the extreme focus on individual autonomy found in the Tea Party movement.

The question is whether this dichotomy is not close to becoming obsolete. In Europe at least, one is bound to wonder sometimes: Have we turned things upside down, and are we moving towards societies that have taken the *worst* from the left: centralism and bureaucracy – coupled with the *worst* of the right: selfishness and greed?

It is important that we be aware of the values and the anthropology (philosophy of what a human being is) upon which we wish to build our societies. To be sure, over time *ideology* as a concept has picked up some very negative connotations – perhaps because many know from experience how rigid systems may prevent flexibility and compromise.

But values and anthropology may also make a positive contribution, providing us with a sense of direction; an inner compass for the individual and a compass to guide society in setting priorities and engaging in the struggles of our time. Such a compass is significant not least when crisis comes knocking and politicians must make choices with a high human cost.

If we as citizens fail to actively choose the values we want influencing our lives and societies, then they will be pushed on us from outside. They may be values such as higher efficiency, more competition, willingness to adapt, all of which stem from an underlying ideology of increased productivity. It may be a growing tendency to account for everything, including human life, in terms of dollars or euros. It may be the management culture of public sectors, where everything is monitored, tested, and evaluated in order to secure the rights of citizens.

There is an alternative

What if there were a school of thought that *does not* attempt to take the best from different ideologies, but which is *in itself* a coherent philosophical whole? An anthropology which acknowledges the individual's search for the good life and which simultaneously holds that it is in relation to other people that this search bears fruit? An anthropology which always puts humans at the center, so that ideology, economics, and systems are all secondary? An anthropology in which life is not measured by productivity or by what is of use to society? An anthropology that has driven and still drives social change all over the world?

The first item of good news is that such an anthropology exists. To be sure, it dates back quite a few years and could use a bit of dusting off – at least in some parts of the world, where it has been neglected for many years. But it is still relevant – perhaps now more than ever – and it holds potential for guiding us through the challenges we face concerning matters both national (such as the renewal of public social security) and international (such as peace, reconciliation, and accountable cooperation).

This is why the anthropology in question is called *personalism*. It was developed during a time when the young nation states had to decide how to treat their citizens. Unlike many other ideologies, personalism does not claim to have an answer ready at hand to all the challenges and problems that we as societies and individuals face. There is no answer book, but rather a collection of principles and guidelines that we may follow when attempting to say how we should treat one another and which role the state and other institutions should play in our societies.

This is why personalism is well suited as a compass in these times, marked as they are by great change in our societies and in the world at large. Globalization, financial crisis, climate change, scarce resources, and new technologies and forms of communication all demand that we make decisions with far-reaching consequences.

Personalism offers some points of departure from which to make these decisions, points that are ambitious, but have also shown their applicability in practice.

The next piece of good news is that this anthropology is not so strange to us. Most of us would recognize practical examples of personalism, only perhaps not being aware of the underlying thoughts and values. For instance, personalism forms the backdrop of some of the greatest events of social change the world has seen over the past fifty years. Martin Luther King in the U.S. and the influential archbishop Desmond Tutu in South Africa were both influenced by a personalist anthropology, as were those who formulated de Declaration of Human Rights after the Second World War.

Likewise, many of the solutions that we intuitively consider sensible are often in tune with a personalist anthropology. One powerful example is found in the legal sphere, where good results have been achieved through so-called victim-offender conferences, which arrange for the perpetrator and the victim of a crime to meet face to face. This is a distinctly personalist way of thinking. Another example, but a negative one, is the nursing sectors of certain countries, where it is broadly agreed that surveillance and documentation have excessively become the order of the day – at the cost of actual care, contact, and conversation.

As we can see, personalism is not merely a philosophy or an ideology that looks interesting on paper. It has proved its worth both as inspiration and as a model for solving problems. In these times when politicians as well as regular citizens lack proper reference points, personalism may serve as a compass to show us the direction in which to move – as societies and individuals alike.

The fundamental values of personalism

Personalism holds a number of fundamental values that are here gathered together into three basic statements.
- *Humans are relational* and in need of a close and engaged interplay with other humans in larger or smaller communities, in order to thrive and develop our potential.
- *Humans are beings that engage*, i.e. beings that freely take responsibility for our own lives, but also for our fellow humans and for the community at large.
- *Humans have inherent dignity* that can never be relativized or diminished, and which our fellow humans and society have no right to suppress or violate.

Personalism thus stands in opposition to both individualism and collectivism (and thus also to the political ideologies of socialism *and* liberalism alike). Personalism emphasizes the individual person's freedom and responsibility for his or her own life, while simultane-

Individualism *Personalism* *Collectivism*

PLACING PERSONALISM

According to personalism humans are relational, dignified, and engaged beings. The dignified and engaged human person comes into existence through relationship with others.

Personalism is thus on the one hand opposed to *individualism*, which sees persons as independent from fellow humans – and on the other hand to *collectivism* which sees persons as subjected to society or community. Personalism emphasizes the individual's freedom and responsibility for his or her own life while simultaneously stressing how humans can practice this responsibility only in relation to others. Conversely, community may never take precedence over the individual.

Personalism is also opposed to a materialist anthropology, which claims that humans are reducible to something biological. Personalism holds that humans are *spirit* as well – not necessarily spirit in a religious sense, but as that which elevates humanity above nature (in the same sense that there used to be in some European languages a distinction between the natural sciences and the sciences of "spirit," which were concerned with "higher things" or with "high culture," conveying the notion that there is a *something more* to human existence, something accessible to the human intellect.)

ously stressing that humans can realize this responsibility *only* in relation to our fellow humans. Some personalists go as far as to say that humans exist only in relationship with others. Personalism can thus never end up in liberalism, since the relationship to other humans and their needs will always have a say in how I am to live my own life.

On the other hand, personalism also stands in opposition to left-wing collectivism by maintaining that community or society may never have priority over the individual. According to personalism, institutions and systems, including states and civil authorities, are only of use in as far as they serve to help individuals unfold their lives. It is therefore not the primary concern of personalists whether the state is large or small, but rather that power be put to the service of humans and that it be decentralized, in order for the individual to have the greatest possible say in the decisions that concern her or him.

Personalism, then, is critical of all systems that incapacitate, alienate, and violate the individual, no matter in whose name these things are done. Systems and institutions should here be taken in the broadest possible sense, including intellectual systems, management systems, and the systems of society at large.

The capacity of humans to engage means that we are able to form and shape our lives through the opportunities and challenges given to us. Human creativity and initiative are resources that are expressed through our personality and can lead to the greatest achievements. According to personalism human potential is inexhaustible since each

THE PERSONALIST ANTHROPOLOGY

- *Humans are relational beings* in need of a close and engaged interplay with other humans in larger or smaller communities, in order to thrive and develop our potential.
- *Humans have the capacity to engage,* a capacity that we realize in freely taking responsibility for our own lives, but also for our fellow humans in local communities and in society at large.
- *Humans have inherent dignity* that can never be relativized or diminished, and which other humans and society have no right to suppress or violate.

WHY IT IS CALLED PERSONALISM

Personalism is a strand of philosophical and political thought which attempts to capture what a human being is – and to then articulate the social and structural consequences. The fact that this anthropology was given the label "personalism" has its historical causes, but primarily it denotes that the human person, and in particular the dignity and engagement and the relationship among persons, is everywhere the point of departure: Humans have inherent dignity, and the good relationship between humans and the engagement of humans in a life of community is essential to the good life and to good societies.[3]

individual will always have the opportunity to influence the community with his or her ideas and creative responses to life's challenges and dilemmas.

Personalism neglected

In most political contexts, personalism is largely unknown. Among personalists, several models have emerged to explain this lack of a breakthrough. In some cases one might say that personalism faded into the background because a suitable blend of collectivist and individualist trends was found – one which was easily mistaken for personalism. Another reason, no doubt, was the competing worldview of *existentialism* which, in Jean-Paul Sartre's version, became so popular as to force personalism off the stage.

But has the content of personalism not been carried over into other strands of thought under a different heading, e.g. social liberalism in some countries? There are several points of similarity, but the peculiar – and decisive – aspects of personalism were not carried over into its replacements, among which is also the so-called "third way" of British New Labour, inspired by sociologist Anthony Giddens.[4] Most importantly, these strands of thought lack an anthropology that would serve as a safeguard against the depersonalization and alienation that continue to show their face time and again.

There are thus many contexts for which the time has come to reintroduce personalism; this is not to claim that this way of thinking will solve all our problems, but rather to suggest that a renewal of our imagination is sorely needed: Is there a different road that we might take? In Europe in particular, a reintroduction of personalism might pertain to the question of the welfare state. It may come as a crucial source of inspiration, given the widespread suggestion that the welfare state, as it was constructed after the Second World War, is nearing the end of its life, and that a replacement must be found.

The thesis of this book

This book's thesis is that we have created a *depersonalized* society – a society which is increasingly moving away from the very basics, from the close relations between dignified humans engaged in their communities, replacing such things with ideology, economics, systems, institutions. The result is an ever greater mistrust of our fellow citizens and of society itself. This mistrust causes a meltdown of society and leaves us unable to handle the serious challenges we face.

This tendency is amplified in a globalized world, where challenges from all over the globe quickly become concrete and present to us all. Our manner of organizing society as separate countries, and as the western world in general, has immediate consequences in remote areas of the world – and vice versa. It is today an inescapable truth that human lives are all interwoven, more so than at any other point in all of history.

The depersonalization that has taken place in society is not part of a malicious conspiracy for which somebody is to blame. It has arisen through the choices – in many cases sensible choices – we as societies have made over the past decades, and in many cases it has crept in quite unnoticed. The mechanisms behind such an almost inevitable development will also be subjected to further enquiry.

Against this backdrop, the book will outline the potential contributions of personalism in this situation into which we have brought ourselves. We will not remain at a theoretical level – a number of examples will be provided as to how a personalist anthropology might influence solutions in a number of political areas. These descriptions should not be understood as complete answers or ready-made solutions, since life is not so easily captured in universal or eternal boxes and categories. Rather, they are windows into a way of thinking that may expand our imagination, and they are examples of how our societies might turn out if together we take steps in this direction.

Throughout history personalist thought has sometimes been described as admirable, but nonetheless written off as too naïve when held up against the harsh realities. This is not a valid objection. It is precisely "naïve" persons that have changed the world – people with the courage in an apparently hopeless situation to imagine another possible path, people like Martin Luther King, Desmond Tutu, and Václav Havel. With such proponents and role models, personalism deserves to be taken seriously and considered afresh.

This book makes no pretense of treating its themes and problems exhaustively. An effort has been made to outline the main points in personalist thought and the direction in which personalist influence might move our societies. I have chosen to a large extent to use the term personalism as if only one, authorized version existed. This is obviously not the case, but in this book the ambition is to introduce the reader to the main current.

The Relational Human
You and I, Alfred

Swedish author Astrid Lindgren's cheeky child protagonist *Emil from Lönneberg* has a thing or two to teach us. Walking back to the farm on a summer's night after swimming in the lake, Emil looks up at his friend, the family's farmhand Alfred, and says: "You and I, Alfred." They walk in silence for a while, and Alfred then replies: "Yes, you and I, Emil – yes, I'd say so too."

This scene, in all its simplicity, illustrates the absolutely central starting point for personalism: the essential belonging together and the relationship between human persons.

As human beings, we do not float freely in the air, independent of one another. We take part in numerous networks and relationships all the time, every single day. From conception to birth, through childhood and youth, over into adult life, parenthood, and into old age, our lives are characterized by relationships. It is quite telling how we designate each other using relational terms: mother, father, brother, sister, grandparents, colleague, neighbor, spouse, buddy, partner, enemy, and friend.

It is through these relationships that our personality is formed, and it is within these relationships that we live our lives. In emphasizing relationships so strongly, personalism acknowledges that although we certainly are unique individuals, we are at the same time – in a positive sense – bound to one another. Humans are relationally connected. We are mutually dependent; we interact and we influence one another.

Not a compromise, but a radicalization

Strictly speaking, all of the above amounts to a truism with which it hard to disagree. But the mere fact that a personalist anthropology is intuitively sensible to many of us does not entail a notable presence in the western world – either in theory or in practice.

Over the past few decades, the debate about values has mainly involved the two great "isms," individualism and collectivism. Whereas the former emphasizes the freedom of the individual, the latter stresses the communal character of the collective. Naturally, there are perpetual attempts to launch a compromise, a third way, taking the best from left and right. Most of these attempts have been characteristically limited by the very things they were defined against, thus failing to become sufficiently comprehensive.

MARTIN BUBER – I AND THOU

Martin Buber (1878-1965) is an Austrian-born Jewish philosopher who has had great influence upon modern Western thought in philosophy, theology, religion, and pedagogy. He is the best-known representative of dialogical personalism. His main work is the book *Ich und Du* (I and Thou), written in 1923.

In 1930, Buber was appointed professor at the University of Frankfurt am Main, but he resigned in protest immediately after Hitler's rise to power in 1933. He then founded a center for the education of Jews, which became of great importance once the German government banned Jews from public education. In 1938, he left Germany and settled in Jerusalem where he became a professor at the Hebrew University.

Whenever personalists have attempted to pitch their way of thinking, they have often been tempted to formulate it as "a third way." However, it is more relevant to place personalist thought outside – and prior to – the political fields and positions that we know, since personalism has its own intellectual baggage, dating far back in time. It is in no sense a pale compromise – a domesticated version of liberalism combined with a watered-down, liberal-democratic variety of socialism. On the contrary, personalism's claim is that neither the traditional right nor the traditional left is radical enough in the proper sense of the word.

To put it differently: Personalism does not stop at the somewhat trivial observation that at the end of the day, it is our most intimate relationships that matter the most. No, the relationship between human persons is the very set of spectacles through which all of human life should be viewed – and a good relationship to one's fellow humans must be our perpetual

---

Buber's anthropology builds upon the premise that humans are always faced with other beings that they can approach in an I-It mode or and I-Thou mode.

For Buber, the relational constellation of I-Thou is a foundational word, which can only be said with one's entire being, unlike I-It/She/He, which can never be said with one's entire being. What is fundamentally at issue here is not an I and a Thou as separate beings, but rather the foundational relationship: I-Thou. I and Thou are integrated into one another, and they are each other's precondition. It is in the founding encounter that the I enters into its immediate relationship with the Thou.

The individual bears within it an inherent Thou, and through this Thou the individual becomes human. By this Buber means to say that it is within a relationship that the identity and self-understanding of an individual are founded and that it is within relationships that life may be lived. The concept of "the inherent Thou" describes the longing, always present in a human person, for other humans. Without the Thou the I would be crippled. Or better yet: There is no I in itself; there is only the I that is relationized with a Thou.

objective, for such relationship is where a life of value is to be found. Personalists believe so strongly in the value of relationships, in the encounter of one human being with another, that they give precedence to it over all other values. All of the above is true not only at a personal level, but also in personalist views about how we should organize our societies.

Relationships in personalism

Personalism's emphasis upon relationships is probably best known as formulated by Jewish-German philosopher *Martin Buber*.

According to Buber, it is the *relationship* with other persons that defines who a person is. The entire life-world of a human being consists of relationships, because humans always take part in relation-

GABRIEL MARCEL – THE BEING-TOGETHER

Gabriel Marcel (1889-1973) was a French philosopher, theater critic, playwright, and musician. He converted to Catholicism in 1929, and his philosophy was later described as a Christian existentialism (e.g. in Jean-Paul Sartre's *Existentialism is a Humanism*) – a label which he first accepted, but from which he subsequently distanced himself.

For Gabriel Marcel, humans are, in his words, *available* to one another. We are beings sensitive to and disposed towards seeking and taking part in relationships.

According to Marcel, the human person is not secured, nor is it even close to being liberated, in a a society shaped by liberalism. Instead it is decidedly narrowed down and restricted. As persons, humans are not opposed to any "we," but to

ships. Even in solitude our thoughts proceed from the context and setting of relationships.

Buber distinguishes between human "I-Thou" relationships and the "I-It" relationship with things. If our relationships are not true, if they are a mere means to achieve an end, what we get is a reified "I-It" relationship to others. And when we regard humans as something else, something less than persons (e.g. clients, customers, or competitors), it becomes easier for us to make decisions and choices that have negative consequences in the lives of those concerned.[5]

Another personalist thinker, philosopher *Gabriel Marcel*, puts it in terms of humans being *available* (disponible) to one another. We are creatures that are disposed towards wanting, seeking, and forming relationships with others. For Marcel, proper human existence is even the anonymous "one" (as in "one wonders why"). According to Marcel, the person can grow only by the perpetual *relationalizing* of one's inherent individuality. One does not become relational by directing one's attention towards oneself, but rather by making oneself available and thereby more transparent, more open, to oneself and to others. Only when humans are no longer "concerned with ourselves," "full of ourselves," are we enabled to receive and embrace another person.

"I become a presence to the Thou, and you become a presence to me. We become irreplaceable to each other," as B.L. Knox puts it in his book about Marcel.[6] In the same spirit, Marcel's book *Homo Viator*, about the metaphysics of hope, declares: "I hope in Thee for us."[7]

In major works such as *The Mystery of Being* and *Man Against Mass Society*, Marcel is also interested in how to preserve the human person's true being and fullness of life in a modern society governed by materialism and technology. In modern societies, the human opportunity "to be," for instance, is threatened by mechanisms of control that focus upon "producing" and "having."

characterized by the positive ties that connect us to others (love, faithfulness, admiration, good will, helpfulness etc.) – as opposed to the loneliness and hostility toward others of inauthentic existence. For Marcel, authentic being is therefore a being-with, a *being-together*.[8]

Another French thinker, *Emmanuel Mounier*, puts it even more strongly, claiming that the person exists only in relation to another person, in that we become conscious of ourselves only through our fellow humans, and we find ourselves only in others: "In its inner experience the person is a presence directed towards the world and other persons, mingled among them in universal space… The *thou*, which implies the *we*, is prior to the *I* – or at least accompanies it… Other persons do not limit it, they enable it to be and to grow."[9]

Against individualism

With its relational anthropology, personalism has distanced itself from individualism, in which relating to one's fellow humans becomes – at best – an optional item in life.

According to personalism, individualism – and its political manifestation, liberalism – commits the error of conceiving of freedom within a relational void. If we think of freedom as merely an individual privilege, we risk limiting the freedom of others through our personal choices. Only when acting out our freedom in a manner respectful of others and in relation to them can we achieve true freedom for all humans. Liberalism supposes that many of our actions do not affect the possibility for others to live out their freedom.

> The *thou*, which implies the *we*, is prior to the *I* – or at least accompanies it… Other persons do not limit it, they enable it to be and to grow.
>
> Emmanuel Mounier

PERSONALISM AS OPPOSED TO INDIVIDUALISM

- Individualism and personalism agree on the inviolability of the human person. However, individualism, according to personalism, underestimates the relational character of humans. In personalist terms, human freedom does not consist in being free from others, but rather in freedom through others. Humans are set free in our obligation and service towards others.
- According to personalism, individualism becomes tyrannical as its premises are those of the strongest.
- Individualism, in organizing itself and society, proceeds from an attitude of isolation and defense, whereas society should, according to personalism, be organized from an open perspective, proceeding from free communities.

An example might be the liberal notion that I am free to accumulate wealth as long as I do not directly harm anyone in my attempts to do so. A personalist objection would then hold that a human person ultimately stands in relationship to all of mankind. Any act of injustice committed in this world is thus a violation of someone's freedom, and therefore also a violation of the freedom of mankind as such, including my own freedom. We should therefore not assert our own freedom without thinking also of the freedom of the Pakistani seamstress or the African coffee farmer.

Even though we do not *directly* stand in relation to the entire world population, we are still bound together by our common humanity. We are all persons, and thus our relationships cannot be reduced to race, ethnicity, religion, citizenship, or any of the labels by which we categorize humans. Globalization has made this somewhat abstract principle quite concrete. Personalism's talk of humans as relational thus requires us to consider carefully the consequences of our local, national, and global politics for our fellow humans regardless of whether the person in question is our neighbor or someone somewhere across the globe.

Personalist *Karol Wojtyla* has carried out extensive studies concerning the connection between individual and relationship. In 1994, he described how individualism is blind to the fact that we as humans experience a richness and a joy when giving ourselves as a gift in charitable love for others: "Individualism thus remains egocentric and selfish. The real antithesis between individualism and personalism emerges not only on the level of theory, but even more *on that of 'ethos.'* The 'ethos' of personalism is altruistic: it moves the person to become a gift for others and to discover joy in giving himself."[10]

The alienation of relationships

KAROL WOJTYLA – ENGAGED UNITY

During his time as a priest and teacher at the University of Lublin, Karol Wojtyla (1920-2005, later to become Pope John Paul II) developed his own personalism, strongly influenced by, among other sources, phenomenology and Max Scheler, as well as by French personalist Mounier. In 1954 he wrote his doctoral dissertation on Scheler.

The fact that Wojtyla developed an ethical personalism was to be of great consequence, as it became fundamental to his work as Pope, thereby also forming the philosophical basis for several decades of the Catholic Church's influence on the world and on millions of people.

The fundamental question that Wojtyla attempts to answer in his work is: What is a human being? A basic theme for Wojtyla is the unity of the human person. He rejects Descartes' dichotomy of soul and body: "In fact, *body and soul are inseparable*: in the person, in the willing agent and in the deliberate act, *they stand or fall together*."[11]

The personalist anthropology with its strong emphasis upon relationships entails that should a human person lose his or her fellow humans – should others become alien or irrelevant – the human person will become alienated from him- or herself. Such alienation occurs because the person's identity and possible ways of self-expression all exist within the relationship, engagement, and interaction with these others. In other words, existential alienation is strictly bound to relational alienation.

The personalist view thus underlines the correlation between alienation in relationships and the alienation of the individual. This emphasis makes the personalist struggle against alienation a struggle

> It is in intentional acts that the person transcends him- or herself; this theme is of paramount concern to Wojtyla, and with him all personalists. Wojtyla explores the theme in terms of humans coming into being through action and thereby entering an ethical life. This dynamic flourishes under freedom and becomes impossible if the human person is employed as a means by impersonal forces.
>
> Wojtyla is deeply indebted to Scheler, however he does not follow him all the way. He finds that Scheler stresses too much the emotional side of life at the cost of the active, will-governed subject. Wojtyla believes that the intellect precedes the emotions. Humans are for Wojtyla an integrated whole that includes both soul and body and comes into existence within community and through intentional action. Humans therefore become alienated if they lose their relationship to, and engagement with, others.
>
> In the Spanish-speaking world, Wojtyla's work has significantly influenced contemporary systematic personalist Juan Manuel Burgos. Based in Madrid, Burgos has developed what he terms a *modern ontological personalism* in which he rigorously unfolds the primacy of the category *person* for any and all philosophical thought about *being*. Burgos, like Wojtyla, seeks to avoid the symptomatic body-mind dualism of modern rationalist philosophy by conceiving of the person as an irreducible triplicity: body, mind, and spirit.[12]

against the distancing, dissolution, and perversion of communities. If the other human in relation to whom I developed my identity should disappear, a part of me will inevitably disappear as well. We are alienated from ourselves if our neighbor becomes alien to us, or if our fellow human has become an unwelcome threat, an *alien*. It is quite telling that the French word *aliéné* means insane: Our mind is so closely connected to others that it becomes sick if the other becomes a stranger. Buber uses the term "mis-encounter" to describe the failure of a real encounter between human beings.

When relationships weaken or are perverted, I lose myself in a profound sense, and I then become a stranger to myself, alienated. Bringing matters to a head, one might say that as far as personalism is concerned, humans exist only in as far as we exist to other humans, or even: "Amo, ergo sum" (I love, therefore I am). We find this sentence in the work of personalists Mounier and Wojtyla.

The ultimate aim for society is therefore the creation of good conditions for relationships, participation, and community. This is the criterion of success for human conditions in modern civilization. Wojtyla radicalizes this notion: "The central problem for mankind in our time, perhaps for all times, is this: *participation or alienation?*"[13]

The precedence of relationships

Personalism, then, claims that humans are by nature disposed towards intimate relationship with others. And furthermore, it is relationship that brings humans the highest degree of happiness – happiness is not to be found in material goods or experiences, but first and foremost in togetherness and community with others.

Most of us may verify this claim by our own experience. The value of relationships surpasses that of material goods, experiences, pleasure, or anything else – all of this is common human experience, and

> "The central problem for mankind in our time, perhaps for all times, is this: participation or alienation?"
>
> KAROL WOJTYLA

when asked what he or she regrets most in life, many a seventy-year-old will reply something along the lines of: I should have focused more on friendship and close relationships.[14]

Such deliberations about the value of intimate relationship often date back to our childhood. Quite a few parents have been asked by their children: "How much would you sell me for?" or something similar. And fathers and mothers then assure their child that there is nothing in the whole world as precious as him or her in particular.

Northern Irish philosopher Peter Rollins points out that our relationships with those closest to us unfold at a level fundamentally different from everything else that we strive for:

"Imagine that most painful of experiences, the loss of our beloved. If we take a moment to reflect upon such a loss in our own life, we find that we do not simply lose something we desire; we begin to lose *the very ability to desire*. The other things that once tempted us lose their seductive power. Thoughts of promotions, vacations, and new homes lose all of their glittering appeal."[15]

Peter Rollins concludes that the ones we love are not mere objects of our desire, but rather the very source of our desire. In this sense, it is *the other* who imparts meaning and significance to our deeds and possessions. The ones we love are more than objects we strive for; they give birth to and sustain our capacity for desire, for engaging the world, for wanting to live.

Happiness is other people

The significance of relationships for human lives is underscored by a number of surveys. Just to mention a few:

A survey conducted by the international Organisation for Economic Co-operation and Development (OECD), shows that the most decisive factor in the good life is community and the relationship with others. Marking its fiftieth birthday, the organization initiated the *Your Better Life Index*, meant to measure well-being in the developed world. A good life is measured by eleven criteria, one of which is satisfaction. According to happiness researcher Christian Bjørnskov, research has shown that people's satisfaction revolves to a great extent around "the relationship with other people."[16]

OECD: HAPPINESS IS OTHER PEOPLE

A survey conducted by the Organisation for Economic Co-operation and Development (OECD), shows that the most decisive factor in the good life is community and the relationship with others.

The website *Your Better Life Index* explains the significance of relationships with others: "Humans are social creatures. The frequency of our contact with others and the quality of our personal relationships are thus crucial determinants of our well-being. Studies show that time spent with friends is associated with a higher average level of positive feelings and a lower average level of negative feelings than time spent in other ways."[18]

According to the OECD, the index is the first concrete result from the so-called Stiglitz report from 2009, which recommended finding ways of measuring a country's success more adequately than the narrowly economic GDP – Gross Domestic Product – which measures only production.

The report is named after Joseph Stiglitz (1943-) who was in charge of its pre-

A great number of scientific studies show a correlation between weak relationships and a higher rate of mortality. One study concludes that weak social relations are as dangerous to our health as smoking fifteen cigarettes a day. "Loneliness is as lethal as smoking, so we need to take it seriously," concludes ones of the world's leading loneliness researchers, John T. Cacioppo. We tend to focus so much on the independence of individuals that we overlook an important social element: being there for others, says Cacioppo, who speaks of high-quality relationships in which one may both give and receive help.[17]

Several studies have also shown that those who receive emotional support have a lower rate of mortality than those who go without this kind of support. The strongest protection comes from *giving* (not re-paration. Stiglitz is professor of economics at Columbia University, former chief economist of the World Bank, and recipient of the Nobel Memorial Prize in Economic Sciences. He is famous for his critique of global free market economists, whom he likes to call "free market fundamentalists," and of what he terms a "GDP fetish."

Stiglitz points out that the traditional narrow economic parameters do not take into account the great indirect effects and costs of production. How desirable is it, for instance, to have high economic growth if a large part of the population fall ill from stress over time because of the way work life is organized? This "stress cost" is an indirect negative effect of growth, but it is not reflected within the traditional narrow focus on the GDP.

"GDP has increasingly become used as a measure of societal well-being, and changes in the structure of the economy and our society have made it an increasingly poor one," says Stiglitz, encouraging innovative thought: "It is time for our statistics system to put more emphasis on measuring the well-being of the population than on economic production."[19]

ceiving) practical support to friends, family, and neighbors, and from *giving* emotional support to one's partner.[20]

Recent studies have shown that the human need for community is deeply encoded in us. Danish neurologist Morten L. Kringelbach says: "The brain is first and foremost a social organ, and the greatest pleasure available to us is being together with other people. Jean-Paul Sartre said that Hell is other people, but at the same time it is clear that the greatest joy is other people. And this joy is perhaps the most important element of our lives. If we want to understand happiness, we need to understand that the brain is something social."[21]

And is this not what Frida Kahlo realizes in the movie *Frida*? The movie is a portrait of the dramatic and artistic love affair between Mexico's great painter Diego Rivera and surrealist painter Frida Kahlo. In the movie, the main characters are reconciled after a long period of separation, and instead of using the more common expression, "I miss you," as if the relationship were about filling out some lack in the self, Frida says: "I miss us" – realizing that their relationship had made them something more than the sum of two individuals.

The decay of relationships

There are, however, strong currents in society that pull us away from relationships, towards individuality and loneliness. We are part of a culture that has been individualized like no other. People have the option of making themselves independent of family and all other social contexts if they so choose. This is why we need personalism's emphasis on human relations as a reminder of our dependence upon one another.

In 1979, Christopher Lasch wrote the book *The Culture of Narcissism* about the development in the western world of societies in which citizens see themselves as the center of all existence.[22] In our day, this development has reached new heights that Lasch is not likely to have

> The brain is first and foremost a social organ, and the greatest pleasure available to us is being together with other people.
>
> Neurologist Morten L. Kringelbach

even imagined. Today we witness a desperate struggle to "be seen" by as many people as possible and to build one's own "brand" in order to appear successful. The highest goal of existence is to achieve one's "fifteen minutes of fame," as Andy Warhol put it. Others become competitors for attention or power, or they become means that we use in order to achieve our goal of the highest possible social status. This tendency creates a social hierarchy in which we are constantly judged according to what we do, how we look, with whom we associate, how much power and influence we have, etc. In a word, our self-realization comes at the cost of others instead of occurring in relation to others.

The desire to achieve social status is obviously nothing new or unique to our time, but a decisive shift has occurred. Whereas before our identity was to a large degree set from the moment we were born and held accountable by our communities, today we are told that we have every opportunity in the world to do exactly what we want – if we seize the opportunity, that is. If not, we have only ourselves to blame. With stress and depression being such prevalent ailments, it seems reasonable to locate the cause within a competitive society where "being in the spotlight" is the order of the day. Modern humans have to deal with and decide upon an infinite number of extremely complicated problems. While these decisions may have great consequences, the gap between our responsibility and our actual influence is wide. Yet when we fail, such failure reflects on us. In the middle of this maelstrom of responsibility and decisions, we are expected to portray and brand ourselves as energetic and successful.

This correlation is supported by psychologists Keith Campbell and Jean Twenge who show in their book *The Narcissism Epidemic* that narcissistic personal traits have become more dominant. They also argue that the growing number of depression and anxiety cases observed in psychiatry has neatly followed the curve of increasing narcissism.

If we look at the figures, narcissism seems to cause everything we used to hope that high self-esteem would prevent," says Campbell, listing "aggression, depression, materialism, and lack of care for others."[23]

The demand for us to create our own "perfect life" puts relationships under pressure. The intimate relationships that used to be firm reference points in life are no longer a given, and a competitive society will, from a personalist perspective, inevitably damage all types of relationships among humans.

STRESS: THE GREAT SYMPTOM

- In 2011/12 there were 428.000 cases of work-related stress in the UK.
- The occupational groups most exposed to work-related stress were those involved in health care, education, and other types of care service, as well as public administration and defense. Health, education, and care professionals also account for the highest prevalence rates for work-related stress.
- These findings regarding occupation are matched for the entire EU by a 2009 risk report from the European Agency for Safety and Health at Work, with the additions of agriculture, fishing, and hunting.
- A 2013 report from the Safe Work Australia agency shows that work-related stress accounts for an overall loss of approximately ten billion dollars for Australian businesses.

It is thought-provoking how the weakening of relationships has taken place during a period in which we have developed and started using more devices of communication than ever before. Many of us regularly interact with more people than was the norm earlier in history. But this does not necessarily entail a strengthening of our relationships. Quite the contrary.

In her book *Alone Together*[24], Sherry Turkle describes how we use social media to achieve some sense of community without having other people get too close to us. This confirms studies showing that social media, such as Facebook, make users feel both more connected to other people and more isolated from other people.[25] It is quite possible for us to have more acquaintances while at the same time feeling increasingly lonely and having a smaller number of intimate relationships.

- In 2007, The Work Foundation reported that stress is the primary hazard of concern for workers in Britain, and that stress is the most costly work-related illness in terms of lost work hours.
- The Health and Safety Executive agency estimate that work-related stress is the cause of 12.8 million reported lost working days per year in Britain.
- In addition to the costly affair of absenteeism (the absence of employees from the workplace due to stress) there is the complementary phenomenon of presenteeism – the loss of productivity in actually present employees due to stress. In 2009, the US independent advocacy Health Advocate estimated that presenteeism costs American businesses close to 150 billion dollars per year.
- The World Health Organization predicts that stress and depression will become the main causes of illness by 2020.[26]

Systemic failure

It is characteristic of personalism not to stop at the individual level. Personalism does not make the weakening of relationships an individual problem, nor does personalism leave it up to human free choice whether or not to invest in close relationships. The depersonalization of western societies is a *systemic failure* – a development within western culture that cannot be fought at the individual level alone.

In his book *Konkurrencestaten* (The Competition State), Danish professor Ove Kaj Pedersen sheds light on some of the mechanisms behind the decay of relationships. He shows a change in Danish society since the 1970s from *a welfare state* to *a competition state*, resulting in a significantly different view of the human person (welfare state meaning not a state in which everyone receives welfare, but rather the European ideal of a state obliged to take care of its citizens as opposed to merely managing or exploiting them):

"The competition state is a state which seeks to hold the individual responsible for his or her own life and which views community as tied to work, and freedom as identical to the freedom to realize one's own needs – instead of stressing (as the welfare state does) moral formation, democracy as community, and freedom as the opportunity to take part in political processes."[27]

Ove Kaj Pedersen believes that the Scandinavian welfare state, as it used to exist, formed in its citizens an *existential personality*, not least inspired by Danish philosopher and theologian K. E. Løgstrup: "The school's task was to teach the individual to become human among humans, something that was possible only if the teacher recognized the individual as something which they were not yet, but which they always and already had the potential to become, namely a human being."[28] In a welfare state, then, the person must be formed in order to accept responsibility for the community.

The competition state, on the other hand, champions the ideal of *the opportunist personality*. The citizen is now to be formed to "regard him- or herself as responsible for his or her own skills and development. Self-realization through work is thus the contemporary task of pedagogy."[29] In other words, it is now professional competence and skills that provide access to personal formation.

If Ove Kaj Pedersen is correct in his analysis, then it is obvious that the conditions for relationship are poor in a competition state, and that recovering strong relationships is not an individual project but a common one. It makes a world of difference whether we teach our children to seek their own interests or whether we (also) teach them to take responsibility for others and for taking part in democracy.

Professor Jørn Henrik Petersen of the University of Southern Denmark is head of a center for research concerning the welfare state. His view is similar to Pedersen's. According to him, the fundamental anthropology of the welfare state has changed dramatically since the beginning of the 1950s: starting from the community-oriented citizen, going through the critical service user, then the egoistic consumer, and now the non-responsible customer.

"What we have traditionally called our welfare state is a society which is to a large degree morally founded. Morally founded in the sense that rights and obligations are tightly bound together, and always have been. I have no doubt that what we call the crisis of the welfare state, which has now come under the influence of our financial troubles, is also, fundamentally, a moral crisis. Quite a lot can be done through economic intervention. We can weaken the conditions for using arrangements that are perhaps no longer suitable, but fundamentally, looking at the core of the problem, it's really about our behavior towards each other, towards society."[30]

Family is not sacred

Given personalism's critical attitude towards the competition state's devaluation of relationships, one might expect it to follow conservative voices in embracing the family with its intimate relationships. And it has done so, historically speaking. But nonetheless, the nuclear family is not the answer to loneliness and the dissolution of relationships. On the contrary, it may be viewed as a step on the road to individualized society.

The nuclear family is not a natural state or some special original habitat for humans. It is, in fact, the sister of individualization. Both phenomena are children of the post-industrialization bourgeoisie, subsequently disseminated to other parts of society. The nuclear family was really a form of disconnecting. The domestic values represented by the family model were *a turning away* from family in the broader sense and *a turning towards* one's very closest relatives. It is therefore worth asking whether the nuclear family is an adequate institution when it comes to generating social cohesion and inclusion.

The significance of intimate, trust-building, formative, and binding relationships is hard to overestimate. But what about those who fall outside? Perhaps it would make sense to turn backwards in order to find our way forward. In ancient Greece the greater family or the household was the basic unit of society. This extended family (the *oikos*) was a house community that included more than just the nuclear family. Before the industrialization, extended families, clans, tribes, and other medium-sized communities were important pillars of society. Together with the structures of close family relations, they formed a tight and natural network of meaningful relationships.

The global economic recession has seen an increase in multi-generational households, especially in western countries. A lot of experimenting is going on worldwide concerning new forms of housing, such as:

> It is a primal drive in humans that if they are aware of having done something wrong, they have a need to say sorry.
>
> COORDINATOR CHARLOTTE WEGENER

cohabitation for the elderly, live-in communities where nuclear families, single people, and other family types live together under the same roof or in separate housing units that share a single kitchen or other facilities.

The best response to loneliness and the dismantling of relationships is not necessarily (nuclear) family politics and (nuclear) family values but rather supporting the development of new forms of cohabitation. This might include a housing politics centered around the extended family, thus providing these larger communities with better opportunities to care for their children and the elderly. Or it might entail making possible the transfer of tax allowances within an extended household. Both changes would work toward making other forms of community equal to the nuclear family's form of habitation.

Relationships in the legal system

Personalists do not view human relationships as merely a means to increasing the individual's quality of life. Instead they believe so strongly in the potential and force of relationships that they see them as crucial tools to work with in a number of social spheres. Naturally this belief pertains to those spheres that are concerned with people, e.g. education, the elderly, health care, and the social sector. Quite an amount of research has actually been done in these areas in which personalist thought plays a significant role.

This pertinence holds for the legal system as well. Some theories about crime view the offender as a victim – a problematic upbringing, poor living conditions, unjust systems, or unfortunate circumstances may turn a person into a criminal. Or in popular terms: Blame society. Others take a more individualist approach, emphasizing the responsibility of the offender and correspondingly downplaying the circumstances.

There may be good reasons for looking at the circumstances that lead people towards a criminal career, but a personalist way of thinking would start elsewhere. In cases of violence, robbery or the likes, there are (at least) two parties involved – the offended party and the party who committed the crime. And within a personalist scope, they are not merely victim and perpetrator; both parties are persons. Both parties should be thought of and treated as humans, with the aim of *restoring relationships* in as far as this is possible.

Our society is built upon the perpetrator's responsibility to the principles of law, whereas less attention is given to the perpetrator's responsibility to the victim. This approach robs both parties of the opportunity for *reconciliation and actual restoration*, including restoration in relation to the community.

One step towards a personalist way of thinking in the legal system is the implementation of so-called victim-offender conferences. Here the offended party is provided with the opportunity to process the unpleasant occurrence by telling the story of his or her experience to the offender. The perpetrator, in turn, can give his or her version of what happened and also has the opportunity to apologize. In the words of Charlotte Wegener, coordinator of victim-offender conferences in Denmark: "It is a primal drive in humans that if they are aware of having done something wrong, they have a need to say sorry."[31]

Some indigenous peoples in New Zealand and Canada, among other places, have an ancient legal system known as *restorative justice* that is built precisely on these principles. Here all those affected by a given crime are summoned in order to agree on a suitable consequen-

> My humanity is caught up, is inextricably bound up, in yours... We are bound up in a delicate network of interdependence because a person is a person through other persons. To dehumanize others inexorably means that one is dehumanized as well.
> Archbishop DESMOND TUTU

ce for the criminal and to restore the relationships involved insofar as such restoration is possible, in a dignified way.[32] In Norway participation in a victim-offender conference is rewarded with a penalty reduction. Such initiatives should not necessarily be copied, but they are examples of how it is possible to unfold a more personalist way of thinking within a legal system.

According to personalism, our legal system, like everything else, should be permeated by dignity, relationship, and engagement. Research has confirmed the usefulness of alternative forms of punishment such as community service or an electronic tag. These forms of punishment are normally used instead of a mild prison sentence. Community service consists in unpaid work at, for instance, a library or a daycare center. The work is scheduled in the convict's time off, enabling her or him to live and work normally. Studies have shown that these alternative forms result in a higher sense of dignity for convicts, securing an unbroken relationship with, responsibility towards, and engagement in their own lives and that of the community.

Reconciliation in South Africa

The same way of thinking was responsible when in 1994, breaking with the apartheid system, the new South Africa established a Truth and Reconciliation Committee which became a great inspiration for solving conflicts elsewhere in the world. The commission was to map the human rights violations that had taken place under the apartheid regime and – what was more revolutionary – attempt to bring about reconciliation among the population groups.

South African Archbishop *Desmond Tutu* was chosen to head the commission, and Tutu has been deeply influenced by personalism in his struggle against apartheid. According to Tutu reconciliation, or personal amnesty, are consistent with a central concept in his own African worldview; something which in the Bantu languages is known as *Ubuntu*, and which may be translated into: "A person is a person th-

**DESMOND TUTU
– RECONCILIATION AND COMMUNITY**

Desmond Tutu (born 1931) is a South African human rights activist and retired archbishop who became famous worldwide for his nonviolent resistance to the apartheid system. Desmond Tutu was born in Transvaal, but his family moved to Johannesburg when he was twelve years old. He first trained to be a teacher like his father and taught for some years. He then went on to study theology. In 1960 he was ordained a priest in the Anglican Church, and in 1986 he became the first black archbishop of Cape Town. He is an honorary doctor at a number of universities in the US and Europe and has received many international prizes.

In 1984, Tutu was awarded the Nobel Peace Prize for his work towards a peaceful transition to majority rule in South Africa. After the fall of the apartheid regime, he became head of the Truth and Reconciliation Committee, which in turn became a great inspiration for resolving conflicts elsewhere in the world.

rough other persons." It is the content of this word that has driven so many to choose to forgive rather than demand retribution – to declare themselves ready to renounce revenge.

"Ubuntu is very difficult to render into a Western language. It speaks of the very essence of being human. When we want to give high praise to someone we say, Yu, u nobuntu; hey, so-and-so has Ubuntu. Then you are generous, you are hospitable, and you are friendly and caring and compassionate. You share what you have. It is to say, my humanity is caught up, is inextricably bound up, in yours."[33]

A person with *Ubuntu* is open and available to others, affirming the personality of others and not feeling threatened by the skill and good-

---

The commission was to map the human rights violations that had taken place during the apartheid regime and, something more revolutionary, attempt to bring about reconciliation among the population groups.

Tutu stresses heavily the value and dignity of humans on the grounds that we are created in the image of God. For this reason he had to fight against an apartheid regime that denied the equal worth of humans. He has subsequently entered the struggle against other forms of injustice and oppression, using non-violent means, with peace and reconciliation as the ends.

Tutu has formulated an African version of personalism, using the concept of Ubuntu. Ubuntu is an ancient African concept that expresses the way in which humans depend on each other.

"We are different in order to know our need of each other. To be human is to be dependent. Ubuntu speaks of spiritual attributes such as generosity, hospitality, compassion, caring, sharing. You could be affluent in material possessions but still be without ubuntu. This concept speaks of how people are more important than things, than profits, than material possessions. It speaks about the intrinsic worth of persons as not dependent on extraneous things such as status, race, creed, gender, or achievement."[34]

ness of others. This is because such a person possesses a fundamental self-esteem because he or she is aware of belonging in a larger context, suffering when others are humiliated or belittled, when others are tortured or oppressed or treated without dignity. "We are bound up in a delicate network of interdependence because… a person is a person through other persons. To dehumanize others inexorably means that one is dehumanized as well," says Desmond Tutu, thus elegantly placing personalism within an African tradition.[35]

A multicultural society

If this sort of reconciliation and togetherness can work in South Africa, then it is also possible in other places. It ought to be applicable to all Western societies, most of which have people from many different cultures and nations living side by side.

One consequence of the depersonalization of society is that we categorize each other into groups. We speak of "immigrants," "foreigners," "fugitives," and "Muslims" in generalizing terms, a rhetoric that forms the basis for prejudice and images of the other as an enemy. It is worth noting that some categories are more prone to create distance than others. For example, some countries tend to speak of "second generation *immigrants*" as opposed to, for instance, "second generation *Americans*."

Many politicians and political scientists find occasion to worry greatly about the social cohesion in their countries. But the solution is not to create a homogeneous society in which everybody has to be like the rest. Social cohesion in a society is about humans engaging responsibly – with respect for each other's differences and building relationships across boundaries. Since personalism views each human being as unique and valuable, integration cannot be about adjusting to an already defined set of cultural norms. Instead, it must be about actively taking part in the community with the culture and the creative skills that one possesses. This is true not only for non-natives; the goal is for every single person in a society to contribute to the common good with his or her capacities and resources.

Summary

What sets personalism apart from other philosophies and views of life is its central focus on the relationships amongst humans. Whereas individualism emphasizes the freedom of the individual, and collectivism emphasizes the togetherness of the collective, personalism stresses the *encounter* among the individuals in a community.

Humans reach beyond ourselves and really do not gain our existence except in relation to others. We are mutually dependent and – in a positive sense – tied together.

Human relationships are central to personalism, and not merely at the individual level. Rather, they form the very frame of reference for looking at all of human life; they provide a valuable foundation for society. We also find in human relationships a potential for solving problems in practically all political spheres.

In modern society, there is a perpetual movement towards *depersonalization*, towards a weakening of relationships. Because of this movement there is a constant need for efforts and initiatives that move society and human communities in a personalist direction.

One might then ask: Won't such a strong emphasis upon humans relating and being bound to each other come at the cost of human freedom? After all, we don't always experience relationships as something positive; they can also seem like ropes to tie us down. Does the personalist anthropology not start from an idealized conception of relationships among humans? This question will be explored in the next chapter.

The Engaged Human
You Are Free for Community

"Hell is other people"[36], claims the founder of modern existentialism, Jean-Paul Sartre, thus positioning himself in direct opposition to personalism – since personalism claims that fundamentally, we can realize our humanity only in relation to other humans.

The fathers of personalism, however, are not blind to the fact that coexistence with other humans can also be problematic. Most people have first-hand experience of relationships as something not entirely positive; they may also become ropes to tie us down. "The world of others is no garden of delight," says Mounier, "it is a perpetual provocation to self-diminishment or aggrandizement."[37]

However, the demanding character of human relations should not make us renounce this "world of others" and withdraw from it, or make of it a tool to further our own agendas. Mounier believes that a "kind of instinct works continually within us to deny or diminish the humanity of those around us."[38] Or to put it differently: We have in us a tendency to depersonalize the humans that surround us. But we will not reach freedom by following this tendency but rather by fighting for true relationships unfolding in freedom.

For personalism there is no contradiction between human freedom and a life of relationship.

On the contrary, true freedom may only unfold within relationship. And my freedom depends on the freedom of others. "I cannot be truly free until everyone around me, man or woman, is equally free… I become free only through the liberty of others,"³⁹ says Mounier, quoting Russian anarchist Mikail Bakunin. It is fundamentally meaningless to speak of freedom merely as independence. If freedom is not used to make a choice, to make oneself dependent on something, to commit oneself, it is worthless. "Freedom it is not only refusal and conquest, but it is also – and ultimately – the act of association,"⁴⁰ says Mounier.

Limits to politics

For personalism, the concept of freedom is not tied to independence from other people, but to freedom from the oppression of systems, structures, and institutions. First and foremost, freedom belongs to-

EMMANUEL MOUNIER – ENGAGED SPIRIT

In Western Europe, French thinker Emmanuel Mounier (1905-1950) developed personalism into a more political and activist movement. In 1932, he founded the periodical Esprit, which became the main outlet for personalism and attained great influence, not least in France.

As a young philosophy graduate in the early 1930s, Mounier was shocked by the financial collapse and the world order that caused such human suffering. This experience led him to the insight that human responsibility is not abstract and impersonal, but very concrete and personal.

Mounier sees the modern civilization as fundamentally derailed by materialism, individualism, and capitalism. He therefore calls for a nonviolent, cultural revolution to pave the way for a "total reconstruction of our civilization."⁴¹ A personalist society, according to Mounier, should aim to guarantee human rights and prevent

gether with responsibility, with human beings taking responsibility for their own situation and for the communities, large and small, that they are part of.

And so it makes sense to begin this chapter on *the engaged human* by emphasizing human freedom. The close correspondence between the two is something most of us probably know from experience; it is wherever freedom is awarded that there is also creativity and engagement. This is true of both large and small communities; it is true of the workplace, it is true of associations and unions, and of family.

And it is true of society at large. A society works well if its citizens are active, responsible, engaged, creative, and prone to take initiative. Personalism therefore emphasizes smaller communities in which hu-

---

the state or other institutions from violating the personal domains of human life. Positively defined, personalism wishes to organize society so as to develop in every level a maximum of initiative, responsibility, community, and decentralization.

Mounier sees the capitalist market economy as a good method for meeting our material needs, but he is an indignant critic of the all-encompassing dominance that capitalism has attained. Liberalism tends, in the name of freedom, to destroy freedom and initiative by handing them over to capitalist oppression. Collectivism protects society from being dominated by a particular interest, but has a tendency to bind freedom and concede power to just one party or social class. Personalism attempts to retain the collective as well as freedom through an economy in which, for instance, big industry consists of self-governing institutions, but within a mandate issued by society.

The program presented by Mounier for analyzing, breaking, and replacing the order of his time is put forward systematically in *A Personalist Manifesto* (1938) and *Personalism* (1952). He stresses that the program does not contain definitive solutions, but rather presents a way of thinking and living. Personalism is not a system; it is a perspective, a method, and a demand.

mans have great influence on their own existence, and on decisions being made as close to the citizens as possible. It is a positive thing when civil society and altruistic volunteer effort flourish.

This is a state of affairs that the economic school of the so-called *distributists*, among many others, has sought to bring about. The best-known proponents of distributism were Roman Catholic thinkers and writers Hilaire Belloc (1870-1953) and G. K. Chesterton (1874-1936). To a large extent, its basis was the social teachings that proceeded from the Vatican, especially that of popes Leo XIII and Pius XI, and it found another proponent in pope John Paul II.[42] Distributism tends to view the home and the family, and thus also local and civil society, as the very foundation of all human society. It seeks to strengthen this basis by distributing ownership, especially the ownership of *means of production*, as widely as possible.

In other words, government, according to distributism, exists not in order to own or control the means of production – as in a socialist state – but rather in order to keep these means from falling into the hands of a few privileged individuals or corporations – as is the case in a capitalist society, narrowly defined. Government thus has the function of securing the economic conditions for a tapestry of autonomous local communities to arise and flourish, based on family and exercise of ownership in one's own spheres of meaningful life.[43]

Grundtvig and freedom

The Danish priest and preacher N.F.S. Grundtvig (1783-1872), an important popular educator, was especially known for his views on freedom and community. "Freedom for the common good" is one of Grundtvig's most remarkable dictums concerning freedom. It refers to the idea that individual freedom should reach only as far as it is possible while still taking social cohesion into consideration. In opposition to "freedom for the common good," we find "unbridled freedom,"

> Freedom it is not only refusal and conquest, but it is also – and ultimately – the act of association.
>
> EMMANUEL MOUNIER

which was Grundtvig's name for the type of freedom that considers only the egoistic interests of the individual, and which therefore does not consider social cohesion.

Grundtvig says of freedom that it is "a word as slippery as an eel," and he is therefore largely unconcerned with finding a precise definition of freedom. Grundtvig's conception of freedom never takes the shape of an abstract idea. Rather it is always tied to concrete historical circumstances in which one is a human being together with other humans. In the periodical *The Dane*, which Grundtvig published from 1848 to 1851, he explains how he accepted election for the constitutional assembly with a certain goal: "the common good as the unshakeable constitution of all constitutions." During his travels to England, he had become acquainted with an economic liberalism that he thought had gone way too far. In England freedom had ceased to refer to *the common good*, and had come to mean unbridled freedom. They had not realized "that man and the people do not exist for the sake of the state, nor for that of agriculture, capital, or the trade balance, but rather the earth and all earthly things exist for the sake of man and the people and should be used for their good," as Grundtvig puts it.[44]

Grundtvig's analyses and admonitions have great resonance in the contemporary debate about liberal democracies and their crisis. And just as Grundtvig raised his voice in strong opposition to the systems of the day, in defense of humankind, the freedom of the human spirit, and the common good, personalism also raises an oppositional voice today: Citizens in 2014 do not exist for the sake of the state, the financial sector, nor the trade balance. It's exactly the other way around!

Democracy as a way of life

The vision for human beings to engage and take responsibility for ourselves as well as for others naturally leads to a concern for developing democracy. Along with Danish theologian and debater Hal Koch (1904-1963), personalism holds that conversation, community, and the understanding of and respect for others are fundamental to democracy. Democracy is not primarily about decisions of the majority; it is a way of life, a social mindset, a way of thinking and of relating to others. In an article from 1946, Hal Koch is concerned with the challenges faced by modern democracy. As a backdrop for the debate about the future, he goes back to the first democratic experiments in ancient Greece, examining why these democracies had collapsed.

N. F. S. GRUNDTVIG
– FREEDOM FOR THE COMMON GOOD

Nikolaj Frederik Severin Grundtvig (1783-1872) was born in the small Danish town of Udby. He followed his father in studying theology and eventually becoming a priest in the national Lutheran church. Besides his clerical career, Grundtvig was elected several times into parliament around the time when Denmark's status as an absolute monarchy ended with the writing and passing of a national constitution.

Grundtvig wrote extensively on Nordic mythology, which he sought to place within the framework of the Christian narrative. He is also responsible for a massive part of the corpus of Christian hymns that are still sung in the Danish churches.

Another very influential section of Grundtvig's work is his writing about

"The state became something remote and lofty at which one aimed demands, and if these demands were met, one was generally satisfied. The demands were peace and security as well as the conditions for building up one's private existence. The thing was that one sought 'happiness', the substance and meaning of life, not in the political community of the people, but in isolated individual existence."[45]

Hal Koch goes on to compare the democracies of antiquity to the modern one:

"I hardly say too much when I say that this danger most definitely threatens our democracy as well. Hence the demand for politicization. This does not necessarily entail joining a party or conducting political activity as such, but it entails an active solidarity in the face of all our

education and pedagogy. He held that the educational system should not primarily seek to turn the nation's youth into learned scholars. Instead, the primary aim of education should be the formation of responsible, engaged humans with a creative vision for their country.

He argued that fixed curricula and rigid testing were an impediment for the human spirit. Instead an environment of responsible freedom must be provided in which human creativity could flourish and bring about the popular formation of a democratic spirit – one that would freely and passionately embrace its national heritage and administer it for "the common good". This "common good" was, for Grundtvig, "the unshakeable constitution of all constitutions" as well as the justification and end of freedom itself. Grundtvig therefore saw true freedom as opposed to "unbridled freedom", namely the aimless and meaningless state of individual autonomy with no regard for community.

Grundtvig thus inspired the so-called *folkehøjskole* (folk high school) movement that still exists today and which gave birth to a number of alternative creative boarding schools focusing upon the creative and democratic formation of students.

common concerns. This implies that one consciously place the interest of the whole at the center and not be satisfied with merely feathering one's own nest."[46]

Democracy under pressure

Even though Hal Koch wrote more than sixty years ago, most of us probably recognize the problem. A depersonalization has taken place – a shift from finding meaning in the relationships of the community to individual happiness. Hal Koch's proposed solution, then, was a politicization of the population – especially the youth – and so it was

WORDS THAT WORK – CONVERSATION OR SPIN?

When democracy takes form as a conversation, it becomes crucial how we use language. Language is a necessary condition for conversation as well as for action and co-action. Language influences relationships. It can give one person power over another, but it can also convey freedom and life values.

We might speak of different types of language; a language of control, a language of power, or a language of freedom. As is dramatically and poetically staged in William Shakespeare's plays (think of Prince Hamlet's elaborate attempts to trick the king into revealing the truth), language is not mere speech – it consists just as much in persuasion, lies, deception and flattery. Language is not only active when we describe matters of fact (scientific facts) or convey information. Language also reflects ethical values and assessments that concern human and social matters.

Political language has undergone change because the increasing influence of television has placed increasing demands on politicians. Politicians have in turn undergone an increased professionalization in the sense that experts, spin doctors, have gained crucial influence on the language and communication of politicians.

Among other tasks, spin doctors serve to cover up and camouflage things so the media will not penetrate into the real – that which is typically quite inconve-

also essential for him to insist that "democracy is conversation." This principle has been under pressure for many years now. We have seen democracies move from being concerned with dialogue towards a more power-oriented democracy of votes. Once more, a shift towards depersonalization.

To be sure, Europe has occasionally seen political situations where the norm was for broad agreements to be reached through negotiation and conversation among many and diverse parties and organization. But there is a strong tendency for democracy to deteriorate into a profoundly partisan scenario with two sharply opposed blocs competing for votes, or even a simple two-party system with each party known

nient. Because they set the agenda to an ever greater extent, spin doctors may, in coordination with external sympathizers, formulate or stage things to the advantage of their politician or minister.

This development raises some fundamental questions about political communication. If political reality may increasingly be formulated and staged by spin doctors, then how does it relate to the reality experienced by citizens? Is there any correlation, or is it only so when called for by the segment analyses, focus groups, and media strategies of spin doctors?

Howard Kurtz' conclusion in his book *Spin Cycle – Inside the Clinton Propaganda Machine* is the obvious one: "There is no reason whatsoever to believe what one reads in newspaper or sees on television. News and media truth emerge through the interplay of media advisors and journalists rather than between the event and the people."[47]

According to Hal Koch, it is "conversation (dialogue) and mutual understanding and respect that are the essence of democracy."[48] If the essence of democracy is to be preserved, then democratic conversation, broadly speaking, is faced with great challenges in finding sustainable norms for political conversation in a modern world controlled by the media. What we need, if not exactly fixed rules, is at least an ideal to hold the political debate up to.

primarily for a few polarized opinions on very specific issues. A strong example of the consequences of two-party polarization was the recent US government shutdown of 2013.

The reasons for this tendency are many and complex, but one of the most important is the way in which politics is influenced by the general picture presented by the media. Very few media – and media consumers – today have any time for long, complicated analyses. Instead, everything revolves around yes or no, for or against, liberal or conservative, right or left. We want to know the result of the elections right away, as soon as the tallying is done – otherwise it's poor entertainment. And thus dialogue across the political spectrum falls silent, and politics instead becomes exclusively concerned with firmly established blocs scrambling to muster the critical number of votes.

Hal Koch argued for a "politicization": each new generation must be engaged politically – must become responsible partakers – in the conversation, life, democracy, and common good of the community. From a personalist perspective it is beyond doubt that democracy is something to fight for. It is not something we are born with. Democracy is not embedded in our genes just because we happen to be born in the so-called Western part of the world. Democracy must be learned over again by every new generation, and each generation must be willing to learn, or democracy will be watered down and lose its popular appeal.

Or it may come to resemble the "tyranny of the majority" depicted by Alexis de Tocqueville in his famous travelling journal *Democracy in America*: "If it be admitted that a man possessing absolute power may misuse that power by wronging his adversaries, why should not a majority be liable to the same reproach? Men do not change their characters by uniting with one another; nor does their patience in the presence of obstacles increase with their strength. For my own part, I cannot believe it; the power to do everything, which I should refuse to one of my equals, I will never grant to any number of them."[49]

Sentiments such as this serve to remind us of the need for a constant, fundamental debate about the principles of democracy.

Democracy and engagement

It is crucial that we not limit democracy to that which takes place at a town council or a parliament. Democracy fundamentally has to do with engaged humans working for the common good in their local community, in their workplace, in children's and youth clubs, in educational institutions, etc.

Where democracy falls into decay, there will be reactions, which are, as such, a healthy sign – regardless of whether one deems the actual reactions or forms of action sensible. A recent example was the movement *Occupy Wall Street* in the US, which is, among other things, a reaction against a democracy that leaves citizens powerless against the transformation of society into a market where big companies buy influence for themselves and where the general significance of money in elections is huge.

Co-determination and engagement must be strengthened and protected by having people participate to the greatest possible extent in decisions that concern their own lives. Hence the need to delimit the impersonal power of systems, whether they be the market, state institutions, or multinational corporations.

Personalism is characterized by a strong focus on the mediating party between the state and the private sphere, namely civil society. Practically all principles of personalism come into play in the communal spheres of civil society – families, associations, and volunteer activities: We find here a focus upon relationship, the engaged person, human dignity and the whole human person, as well as a break with systematic thought.

A strengthening of civil society could play a major part in reforming current political systems. There are not only economic reasons to do this – it would also inhibit depersonalization and bring the individual into play as an engaged citizen. This basic insight has led many debaters to suggest that governments actively promote and organize civil or national service, perhaps even making it mandatory for citizens.

When *Time* Magazine editor Richard Stengel made his case for universal national service, he started from the pessimism of the founding fathers concerning the future of their newborn republic: "A republic, to survive, needed not only the consent of the governed but also their active participation. It was not a machine that would go of itself; free societies do not stay free without the involvement of their citizens. Today the two central acts of democratic citizenship are voting and paying taxes. That's basically it. The last time we demanded anything else from people was when the draft ended in 1973."[50]

Stengel observes in young Americans a yearning to engage in civil society, making an effort to parallel that of soldiers abroad. He sug-

SOCIAL CAPITAL – THE COHESION OF SOCIETY

If citizens place great trust in each other, return favors, and create civil networks, then the country has what is called social capital. Social capital is a resource for society, along with physical capital and human capital; and it is just as important for social, political, and economic life.

Social capital is defined, according to professor of political science Robert Putnam (1941-), according to norms such as "social trust," "norms of reciprocity," and "networks of civil engagement." Social capital is the factor through which cooperative communities are created, maintained, and developed among individuals, and the number of volunteer unions and associations is therefore the simplest parameter for determining the social capital of any society.[51]

Putnam also designates social capital as a citizen mentality. According to Putnam, social capital is built and consolidated over a long period of time through

gests that the government channel and organize this will to serve, thereby creating a major project of formation that would revive the role of civil society in shaping and upholding the democratic system.

Trust or control

The emphasis on the significance of engagement also influences another field, namely the relationship between trust and control. Wherever there is a low level of trust among citizens, or where the state or local administration places little trust in citizens, trust is replaced by bureaucratic surveillance and control. For instance, employees may be required to check in frequently for the employer to be aware of their whereabouts at any time. Various care institutions may be required to document their every move, rigid standards may be imposed upon school curricula, etc.

---

a long and sensitive process; whereas it quickly deteriorates into mistrust, lack of mutual responsibility, and weak networks. Social capital is a resource for society just like physical or human capital, but unlike physical capital, social capital can be said to be a collective good.

In a word, social capital is a parameter by which to measure the extent to which the citizens of a given society are able to complete tasks collectively. Social capital thus plays an economic role exactly, or at least partially, like physical and human capital. A country that is rich in human and physical capital but poor in social capital, will not function optimally.

It is essential for cooperation among citizens in a greater area that trust not be strictly personal, but also social, i.e. including persons one does not know personally. In societies with great mutual trust, individuals will be less inclined to demand "here-and-now" compensation for accepting obligations in various areas.

For personalism, trust is fundamental – obviously not implying the abolition of control. A society cannot, fundamentally, function without trust. All things being equal, we must on a day-to-day basis expect others to act in a manner that is not harmful to us, even though we know we can never be absolutely sure.

There are rotten eggs in all professions, and every time an example of improper use is brought forth, there is a temptation to introduce new measures of surveillance and control. To be sure, this may have its place in some cases, but increased control easily becomes a vicious cycle to move into. A high degree of control entails an expectation that people will cheat if they can get away with it – that humans will, as preached by neoliberalism, act with rational self-interest. This becomes a self-fulfilling prophecy. And more control means less engagement.

American personalist Thomas O. Buford has written a book about the role of trust for personalism. Buford uses the example of the 9/11 attacks in New York City to illustrate how an all-emcompassing traumatic event brings out the fundamental contrast between fear and trust as governing forces in a society: "Bound by a common fear, we feel singled out, confused, and unstable. Reflecting on the emotions and events that prompt them, we become aware that our culture rests on a relation central to his life, trust. When trust is present we have a basis of community, of hope, and of goals. When it is absent or significantly diminished, fear of others enters accompanied by isolation, instability, and confusion over norms that govern our lives."[52]

Life as and among citizens

The EU Commission designated the year 2011 as the European Year of Volunteering – or in EU terms "The European Year of Voluntary Activities Promoting Active Citizenship." The commission justified its decision by saying that active citizenship is a significant ingredient when it comes to strengthening togetherness and developing democracy.

> Democracy can never be secured, precisely because it is not a system to be implemented but a way of life to be acquired. It is a mindset that must be imparted to each new generation.
>
> Hal Koch

The commission even calls volunteer work one of the key dimensions of active citizenship and democracy, because, to mention just a few reasons, volunteer work makes for valuable learning experience, provides an opportunity to develop social qualifications and skills, and contributes to solidarity.

It is doubtful whether the EU initiative had any practical significance, but it was an attempt to shift the overall focus. Contemporary political debate tends to view the relationship between the market and the state in a narrow, two-dimensional way. It is, however, beneficial to zoom out and make an historical and value-based attempt to discern the difference between ends and means where human well-being is concerned.

If I knew that I had only one more month to live, how would I spend my time? Probably very few of us would make the job market or state institutions a priority. Instead, we would focus on intimacy and experiences together with people we have strong relationships with, and on the groups and communities in which we are involved on a volunteer basis and which reflect our fundamental values. Our workplace and the municipal office help secure our livelihood, but they are not an aim in themselves. They do not bring existential fullness to life. Intimate relationships and voluntary communities do.

There is a constant danger that the effort to secure jobs and the rights of employees become synonymous with opposing volunteer work. Trade and labour unions are easily caught up in a state- and market-based way of thinking. All too often the result is that the willingness of parents or other relatives to lend a hand at the school or nursing home is seen merely as a threat to the professional efforts of jobholders. This is a broad example of how an impersonal structure may ideologically hold civil society at bay and cause it to wither away.

Voluntary associations

Hal Koch, the Danish theologian and debater, saw volunteer-based life in unions and associations as the very nerve of democracy. According to Koch, volunteer associations are the best place to democratize children and young people. In the small democracies of associations, children and young people are formed into democrats (in the proper sense of the word), thus becoming active citizens in the greater democracy. They learn to appreciate values such as conversation, respect, engagement, a social mindset, community, and responsibility.

VOLUNTEERING

According to official US government data, 64.3 million Americans volunteered through a formal organization in 2011. All in all, the volunteer effort of 2011 amounts to 7.9 billion hours of work at an estimated value of 171 billion dollars. One could then go on to calculate the number of full time positions it would take to pay for this amount of work.

Apart from the calculable community value of volunteer work, there are also personal benefits to volunteering. A survey carried out by TimeBank through Reed Executive showed that among 200 of the UK's leading businesses, 73% would prefer a candidate with volunteering experience to one with none. Furthermore, the study revealed that 94% of employees who volunteered in order to add to their

"Democracy is not some dogma to be lectured, or which one could adopt overnight. It is a way of thinking, a way of life which is first acquired by living it in the narrow sphere of private life, relating to family and neighbors, next relating outwards in a broader social sphere, in relation to fellow countrymen, and finally in relation to other nations... Democracy can never be secured, precisely because it is not a system to be implemented but a way of life to be acquired. It is a mindset that must be imparted to each new generation. This need is what makes popular enlightenment and education the very nerve of democracy."[53]

This tradition and view of democracy stresses substance rather than form. It is the substance of democracy – common values and humans with democracy as their attitude in life – rather than technical and formal rules for voting, that is its essence. Public education, unions, and volunteer work can secure the substance for the democratic attitude of citizens.

---

skills had benefited substantially: Either they had gotten their first job, improved their salary, or been promoted.[54]

In 2008 the European Parliament issued a recommendation concerning volunteer work and organizations. The report stated that more than 100 million EU citizens are involved in some sort of volunteer work.[55]

The UN has estimated that the average economic contribution of volunteer efforts amounts to 2.5 percent of the GDP.[56]

Furthermore, research has shown that any society's social capital is primarily accumulated through civil society.[57]

These results suggest that popular education, volunteering, and volunteer organizations produce democratically minded people as well as forming concrete value and skills.

Responsible choices

According to personalist thought, humans form and unfold our personalities through the choices we make and the actions we carry out in life. Personalism is a *philosophy of engagement* in which a person forms and realizes him- or herself through engagement, participation, and action. Every time we choose, we develop a certain aspect of our personality at the cost of other options, thus becoming the people we happen to be – or the people we choose to be.

Naturally, culture, nurture, and our environment play major parts as well, but through our actions and our choices we shape our personality in a very special way – we become unique persons with a unique personality. And when we act, we become responsible humans whom others, all directly or indirectly influenced by our choices, may hold accountable for our actions.

One of the main figures of personalism, Emmanuel Mounier, was a contemporary of Jean-Paul Sartre and had many discussions with the existentialists. Personalism is a form of philosophy of existence, starting from the fact that I exist here and now and that I am part of a world with which I must necessarily engage.

In Sartre's thought, this fundamental condition of life caused an intolerable feeling of nausea – humans are thrown into the world,[58] condemned to freedom and forced to take responsibility for our own actions.

Mounier's fundamental mood is completely different. Despite the vulnerability and suffering of human life, to which he is far from blind, life fills him with joy, with a feeling of inexhaustible richness. The aim of human life is then to partake of this richness, to keep it alive, and to perpetually conquer it.

Personalism, then, views life and the necessity of action as an opportunity, whereas for Sartre, it is rather a curse from which humans cannot escape.

PERSONALISM AS OPPOSED TO EXISTENTIALISM

- Existentialism[59] views the surrounding world as meaningless and hostile, whereas personalism sees the world as fundamentally meaningful. The world and other humans become hostile and meaningless only if one takes away engagement and relationships.
- Whereas for existentialism the Other is an enemy, something that hardens, objectifies, and takes possession, personalism sees others as friends, allies whose relational role sublimates and realizes the human person and creates communities.
- For existentialism, the goal and the norm is freedom; for personalism, it is the good of individual, community, and society alike.

The ultimate aim for human society is therefore to create good conditions for relationship, participation, and community. This is the criterion for success in modern civilization. Wojtyla puts it sharply: "The central problem for humankind in our time, perhaps for all times, is this: *participation* or *alienation*?"[60]

Greatness in small things

When we look at today's world and the seemingly unmanageable challenges and problems we face, it is tempting simply to disconnect and let life go on as usual. Acting and engaging is much more demanding than not doing so.

Furthermore, technological advances mean that we now have access to an endless flow of information about events all over the globe, and it is quite simply easier not to be concerned with famine, global warming, wars and conflict, natural disasters, torture etc. The list of things with which one "ought to" engage seems endless. If one does choose to engage, there is a great danger of being overwhelmed by the scope and complexity of the problems.

In the personalist tradition, all our choices and actions are significant because they make us the persons we are, and they determine our attitude towards the world. Even the smallest everyday decisions are important because they set the direction of our lives.

And so we may start by making decisions and act according to our conscience on a small scale in the knowledge that our choices will influence our own lives as well as the immediate communities we are part of, and ultimately also the larger global community.

This way of thinking is captured by the following saying, usually

SOLITAIRE – LOSE YOUR LOVE THROUGH INDIFFERENCE

The song *Solitaire* was written by American pianist and songwriter Neil Sedaka (1939-) and has been interpreted by artist as diverse as Elvis Presley and Westlife.

The song portrays a lonely existence, metaphorically trapped in a one-man game, solitaire, in which all roads in life lead to depersonalization. The solitary player loses his love through his indifference to others, and because he does not share his heart.

Life unfolds in a whirl all around him, and with it the opportunity to play with others, but he plays his one-man game alone, a game in which he can never be anything but the loser, never unfold his true relational, royal nature. In life's solo game, life goes up in smoke.

> There was a man, a lonely man
> Who lost his love, thru his indifference
> A heart that cared, that went unshared
> Until it died within his silence
> And solitaire's the only game in town

ascribed to American author and philosopher Ralph Waldo Emerson: "Sow a thought and you reap an action; sow an act and you reap a habit; sow a habit and you reap a character; sow a character and you reap a destiny."

The future is not predetermined; it is shaped by the daily choices made by the world's seven billion inhabitants. If we make the right decisions concerning smaller things, we will also find out how to engage with bigger things in a constructive manner.

Now the big question is which actions are right in a given situation. For this there is no answer book. Life is not so simple as to be reduced to general principles. An act that may be right in one situation may be

---

And every road that takes him, takes him down
While life goes on around him everywhere
He's playing solitare

And keeping to himself begins to deal
And still the king of hearts is well concealed
Another losing game comes to an end
And he deals them out again

A little hope goes up in smoke
Just how it goes, goes without saying

There was a man, a lonely man
Who would command the hand he's playing

And solitaire's the only game in town
And every road that takes him, takes him down
While life goes on around him everywhere
He's playing solitaire

fatal in another. But this uncertainty about our choices and their consequences should not lead us into passivity. The uncertainty concerning motivation and visible consequences where action is concerned takes nothing from the fact that humans are made to act and make decisions, to live our lives to the fullest. A dubious decision is therefore ultimately better than no decision, just as an imperfect answer is better than silence and resignation. For Mounier, this attitude to life is crystallized under the heading *affrontement*, the human duty to stop and confront the tasks brought on by life.[61]

Summary

Personalism is a philosophy of engagement, starting from the fact that I exist here and now and that I am part of a world which I must necessarily engage. According to personalist anthropology, humans shape our personalities through the choices we make and the actions we carry out in life. Every time we choose, we develop a particular aspect of our personality at the cost of other options, thus becoming the persons we are, or the persons we choose to be.

The freedom to take responsibility for one's own life and for life in the community is essential for humans to become meaningfully and creatively engaged.

A society works well if its citizens are active, responsible, engaged, creative, and full of initiative. This is why personalism emphasizes smaller communities where humans have greater influence upon their own existence, as well as insisting that decisions be made as close to the citizens as possible. It is also a positive thing for civil society and volunteer-based, altruistic initiative to flourish.

Based on all this, personalists are concerned with developing a democracy that must constantly be re-conquered and revitalized by new generations in order to survive. For personalism, conversation as well as respect for and understanding of others are fundamental to democracy. Democracy is not primarily majority decisions, but rather a way of life, a social mindset, a way of thinking and relating to others.

The Dignified Human
You Are One of a Kind

Instinctively, many of us are uncomfortable with being reduced to a number. This sentiment is often made manifest in popular political resistance to concepts like the social security number. Such resistance is found under administrations that make use of social security numbers, and in other cases, such as the UK, the state itself is reluctant when it comes to reducing citizens to a number.

Our reaction against being reduced to a number probably has something to do with the fact that in some sense it depersonalizes us. It makes us something less than human. This tendency is most clearly manifested in military organization, where soldiers have traditionally been issued a number because they are precisely not a *person*, but a tool without a will of its own, merely intended to obey orders.

When we are depersonalized and become merely a number in the system, we find that we lose part of our human dignity. We believe that we are something *more* than a client, customer, patient, soldier, or whatever it is that the system reduces us to. For the same reason, we react when our value is counted in dollars and cents, or when the later stages of human life are described by something as impersonal as the *old age dependence ratio*. French personalist *Emmanuel Levinas* proposes the view that we must always treat "the Other," our fellow human, as an infinitely valuable person. We must never reduce "the Other" to something completely transparent or identical to ourselves. As soon as we reduce humans to something less than infinitely valuable and unique persons in themselves, we are heading down the same dangerous dead end street that in the twentieth century led to totalitarian regimes, racial hygiene, two world wars, and the Holocaust. According to Levinas, the inviolable dignity of humans becomes apparent when we meet them and see them face to face.⁶²

Many of us intuitively ascribe dignity to others. We might for instance say that the elderly are treated in an undignified manner if they are not decently cared for by the nursing institutions. And we may be of the opinion that people and institutions can behave in a way that *violates the dignity of others*.

EMMANUEL LEVINAS
– THE OTHER AS INFINITE

Emmanuel Levinas (1906-1995) was a Lithuanian-French and Jewish philosopher who took up the mantle of dialogical personalism. He first studied Husserl and Heidegger in Freiburg during the 1930s, attempting to integrate the two philosophers, and later in Sorbonne under the guidance of, among others, Jean Wahl (1888-1874) and Léon Brunschvicg (1869-1944) whose humanism and belief in the moral progress of humanity were to influence Levinas.

The Second World War, during which Levinas was captured and held for four years in a German prisoner camp, became a turning point and a point of orientation throughout the rest of his life. During the war, Levinas' entire family was eradicated, and just as early dialogical personalism was deeply influenced by the First World War, his thought was shaped by his experience of the Holocaust. Against this background, Levinas developed a hope for the redemption of hu-

The inherent dignity

Personalism heavily emphasizes this inherent human dignity. Each human being is unique and cannot be devalued. The human person is inviolable and must never be subject to any form of abuse. When people or systems violate persons, they thereby depersonalize them and treat them like things of no value apart from the one that they violently ascribe to them.

On the contrary, claims personalism, humans are valuable in ourselves, and every single human must therefore be treated with respect, regardless of ethnicity, culture, religion, and social status. All humans, manity through a philosophy that invariably acknowledges an absolute demand that one respect the other's dignity.

In his autobiographical essay *Signature*, Levinas observes that his biography is "dominated by the premonition and the memory of the Nazi horrors."[63]

After the war Levinas developed an original personalist ethic concerned with the interpersonal relationship, culminating in his main work, *Totality and Infinity* (1979). The title refers to the absolutely central aspect of the Levinasian demand, that *the Other* – a fellow human – has *infinite dignity* and is unique in his or her *otherness*, which is why the other always resists our usual attempts to subject the entire word to just one perspective, namely that of the self. Through analyses of the phenomenology of the face, he attempts to show how the ethical demand is concretely manifested in the life of a person.

This work, based upon phenomenology and Jewish humanism, draws on early dialogical personalism. Levinas radicalizes the I-thou relationship, making it the very meaning of existence. The face is given a metaphysical dimension as the demand that one care for or about the other as *Other*. This encounter with *the Other* becomes the authentic and infinite aspect of human existence.

without exception, have a unique personality and may contribute in countless ways to make the world a slightly brighter place. Each person paints with his or her own color on our common canvas.

How may this unique dignity be founded? Historically, the human worth has first been religiously founded: Humans are infinitely valuable because we are created by God, because our creator has made us something special. Humans have, so to speak, received our value from a higher power.

Personalism, however, has made an effort to found the dignity of humans in a secular manner, without religious explanations, starting from, among other sources, German philosopher Immanuel Kant's (1724-1804) thought. For Kant, it is central that one distinguish *price* (German: Preis) from *dignity* (German: Würde). Where things are concerned, we speak of a market price that depends upon supply and demand. The price of a thing reflects its function and potential for meeting an end of ours. The value of a thing is thus viewed in relation to its potential as a means to and end outside the thing itself. But what about human beings? Do they have a price as well? No, says Kant. It would be wrong to conceive of a human as merely a means for the ends of others. Humans can therefore not be said to have a price in the same sense as things do. The human person is an end in him- or herself. Humans therefore have dignity, which is something fundamentally different from a price. For Kant, human dignity is tied to autonomy, i.e. the free right of the rational human, meaning that a human person may not be forced by others, may not be reduced to being merely a means for another's end: "In the kingdom of ends everything has either a *price* or a *dignity*. What has a price can be replaced by something else as its *equivalent*; what on the other hand is above all price and therefore admits of no equivalent has a dignity."[64]

In his book *What is a Person*, American professor of sociology Christian Smith argues that the human person is more than his or her own qualities and capacities. Human dignity cannot be founded in the fact that unlike animals, we are rational beings or capable of moral action. If this were the case, someone in a state of coma would lose his or her dignity.

Smith believes that humans have a personality, a center, situated at another level than the sum of our capacities and qualities, just like water is certainly the sum of oxygen and hydrogen while simultaneously transcending these components.[65]

Humans are spiritual beings

What Smith calls the human personality or center, personalists have traditionally designated as the human *spirit*. Because personalism has arisen alongside the breakthrough of a materialist anthropology, personalists have stressed that the human being is more than nature, namely a "spiritual being."

How would a personalist understand this concept? In a narrow religious sense, the concept of *spirit* covers the human quality that enables us to stand in relation to a God or higher being. Personalists, however, often use it to designate the fact that the spirit unfolds what is exclusively human or personal by rising above the merely animal. In some European languages, this sense of *spirit* is apparent in the notion of the "sciences of spirit" (i.e. *the arts*) as opposed to the natural sciences.

When personalism speaks of humans as spiritual beings, this means that humans, who are partially subject to nature, may rise above nature – behave like cultivated beings of spirit: persons. To a personalist view, those ideologists who reduce humans to being exclusively a fragment of nature commit the fatal mistake of depersonalizing the human.

Russian personalist Nikolai Berdyaev speaks of a human dualism of spirit and nature. Spirit is a free and integrating activity in all humans. The spirit has the right to total freedom and is the foundation for the human person, but the spirit is also inevitably at odds with nature and the aspects of humanity that are determined by physical laws. This anthropology explains Berdyaev's struggle for freedom of spirit and against materialism.[66]

When humans in the western world today are reduced to something less than persons, personalists see this as corresponding to a materialist worldview. If we are not viewed as spiritual beings as well, we are quickly reduced to being consumers and a labor force. The result is the heavily dominant system that we are now subject to, a system that tries to make us believe that the road to happiness consists in producing and consuming.

JACQUES MARITAIN – INTEGRATED HUMANISM

Jacques Maritain (1882-1973) was a French philosopher and, over the years, a professor at several universities in Europe, the US, and Canada. He was a prominent personality within Thomism, a philosophical tradition deriving from the thought of St. Thomas Aquinas, which has been a central element of the Roman Catholic Church's official philosophical foundation since the late 19th century. He made significant contributions to all the basic philosophical disciplines, from epistemology and political philosophy to aesthetics and philosophy of religion. Maritain argued for what he called *integrated humanism*. He held the view that if the spiritual dimension of being human is denied, we then have not a whole, but merely a partial humanism that ignores a very basic aspect of the human person.

Maritain believes it to be both possible and desirable for religious people and

The human family

Personalism is an echo of the idea that humans have dignity in ourselves – and this idea is coupled with the idea of human community, the relationship with others: While humans are unique persons with inviolable dignity, we are also connected to and engaged in communities – or brotherhoods, in the words of the UN human rights declaration: "All human beings are born free and equal in dignity and rights. They are endowed with reason and conscience and should act towards one another in a spirit of brotherhood" (Article 1).

It is far from a coincidence that there is such harmony between personalism and the anthropology of the UN human rights declaration.

---

humanists to cooperate in the political sphere. Both usually agree on the value and importance of love for one's neighbor, service in truth, and the dignity of the human person. According to Maritain and Thomism, these values correspond to the perception of reason and the primary dispositions of our nature. Even though they are deduced and conceived of differently by those with varying convictions, the agreement on the basic tenor and implications of these values is real, and it enables cooperation in the practical sphere.

The acceptance of pluralism and tolerance was thus central to his vision, and Maritain therefore gained respect in a number of contexts. He played a significant role as one of the architects behind the UN human rights declaration of 1948.

Maritain had a close relationship with another great figure in French personalism, Emmanuel Mounier. Both were convinced that the current civilization was subject to a crisis and that a new kind of humanism was needed. Mounier was strongly influenced by Maritain's thought, and more specifically: by his Thomist anthropology, his demand for active social engagement, and his view of society and political philosophy.

French personalist and philosopher *Jacques Maritain* was instrumental in formulating this fundamental declaration about humans and our rights.

This brotherhood or family, the human community (of fate), means that when one human is oppressed or violated, all of humanity is concerned. If a single human life is regarded as expendable, then all human lives are expendable. My dignity entails the dignity of all my fellow humans.

THE UN AND BASIC PRESUPPOSITIONS OF HUMAN WORTH

The UN and all of its projects are based on fundamental presuppositions about humanity, presuppositions that to a great extent reflect a personalist outlook. This is expressed beautifully in Article One of the UN human rights declaration of 1948: "All human beings are born free and equal in dignity and rights. They are endowed with reason and conscience and should act towards one another in a spirit of brotherhood."

Human freedom, equality, dignity, right, reason, conscience, action, and the spirit of brotherhood, these are the fundamental principles of all work within the UN, and everything else is unfolded starting from this anthropology.

If we hold the UN's anthropology up against that of personalism, the likeness is remarkable:

Value: Humans possess rights as well as freedom, equality, and dignity.
Relationship: Humans ought to act in a spirit of brotherhood.
Engagement: Humans ought to act.
Spirit: Humans possess reason, conscience, and the spirit of brotherhood.

In the preamble to the UN Universal Declaration of Human Rights, the point is stressed that "recognition of the inherent dignity and of the equal and inalienable rights of all members of the human family is the foundation of freedom, justice and peace in the world."

From ancient times on, this fundamental view of human dignity and connectedness has found expression in proverbs and sayings. The best-known one is probably Jesus' dictum: "Do to others as you would have them do to you." Immanuel Kant expressed the same matter in his famous categorical imperative: "Act only according to that maxim whereby you can at the same time will that it should become a universal law without contradiction."[67]

It is a pervasive idea in European culture and in personalism that humans occupy a privileged position in nature – a special creaturely dignity. This important idea was a premise for French personalist Jacques Maritain, who wrote the draft for the human rights declaration of 1948. For the international community, the declaration became an important reaction to the totalitarian regimes of the 1930s, and not least to the Nazi violations of human dignity.

In the declaration that "All human beings are born free and equal in dignity and rights," the basic dignity of a human is not tied to particular properties that humans may possess to a smaller or greater extent.[68] On the contrary, the individual possesses dignity simply by virtue of his or her humanity. This dignity is inherent, and it is tied to membership of the human family.

Maritain contributed to the UN Declaration of Human Rights from the vantage point of personalism, but as he describes in his book *Man and the State* from 1951, there was widespread agreement concerning the content of the declaration.

Personalists have since sought to provide a philosophical formulation of the rationale behind the statements simply made in the Declaration. Such an attempt has been made by American personalist Thomas D. Williams, whose work includes the effort to found the Declaration's notion of dignity, seeking to formulate dignity as the key aspect of an ontology of the human person. In Williams' thought the ontological category of dignity becomes crucial in bridging the gap between metaphysics and ethics – i.e. between the fundamental properties of the universe and the way humans ought to act in life and society.[69]

The abstract and the personal

One widespread argument against human rights holds that it is not for humans to pose universal rules for all humanity. This is often coupled with a nationalist conception of people and culture and is directly opposed to the personalist idea that human togetherness across national borders and other boundaries is an inalienable value. Human brotherhood and sisterhood does not stop at the border; it transcends all cultural, religious, and national boundaries. Only when we see the infinite value of all our fellow human beings do we understand our own worth.

Even though we do not have *direct* relationships with the entire world population, we are still bound together by our common humanity. Because we are all persons, our relationships cannot be limited to race, ethnicity, religion, citizenship, or other labels according to which we might divide up humanity. It is therefore necessary for us to consider carefully the consequences of our local, national, and global politics, because these will be consequences for *persons* like ourselves.

Only once we regard others as persons with a face will we realize that we "hold their lives in our hands" – drawing on Danish theologian and philosopher K. E. Løgstrup's expression. Løgstrup uses the concept of *interdependency* (mutual connectedness) to designate how humans are each other's world and destiny because our lives are entangled in and dependent on one another. We can either further or impair the unfolding of each other's lives, and the difference between furthering and impairing can be viewed as the difference between good and evil, right and wrong.

"The individual never has to do with another human without holding some of his or her life in his hand. It may be very little, a transient mood, a readiness which one causes to wither or which one awakes, a loathing which one elaborates or dissolves. But it may also be terribly much, so much that it is up to the individual whether or not the other's life will succeed or not… We are each other's world and each other's destiny."⁷⁰

Italian writer Claudio Magris looks at the relationship between the abstract and the concrete in his description of the thousands of people who have drowned in the Mediterranean, attempting to reach Europe.

"It is understandable that our emotions make us weep over a friend whom we care about and not over a stranger. But we have to know – not in an abstract, but in a real sense and with all our capacity for understanding – that humans whom we have never met and loved are just as real. Therein consists the difference between reactionary thought and democracy. A reactionary will easily mock abstract humanity and the abstract love of the human race because he is capable of loving those of his own class, but not really of understanding that those of the same class as someone unknown to him are just as real: They are not abstractions, but flesh and blood."⁷¹

Norwegian writer Karl Ove Knausgård deals with the same matter when writing about the memorial service in Oslo's Cathedral after the tragic shooting at Utøya in July 2011, where prime minister Jens Stoltenberg read out the names of the victims. "A cry is heard – a cry which has been heard in the world for as long as humans have existed. But the cry did not come when the names were read. The human is concrete," says Knausgård and goes on to question the way we remember names.

"We remember the name of the perpetrator. We remember the name of the Oklahoma bomber, the leading Nazis, the murderers from Srebenica, but not the names of the victims. Here, we merely have the numbers, which creates distance. It was this distance that Stoltenberg dissolved when reading out the names in the church. And without distance, one cannot kill. No one can kill a human being that one looks in the eye. Jews, Muslims, these one may kill, victims robbed of their identity. Then they are merely bodies and numbers."⁷²

This is why it makes such a great impression on us when a museum like Yad Vashem in Jerusalem make such an effort to collect information and testimonies concerning every single person that was killed during the holocaust. A similar effect is achieved at the US Holocaust Memorial Museum in Washington DC, where visitors walk through a section that lists Holocaust victims by their first names, thus provoking identification at an individual level. In this way, they personalize their exhibition. The visitor is made to understand that the victims are not nameless numbers, but humans made of flesh and blood, with hopes and dreams for themselves and their lives.

A system with a life of its own

Aldous Huxley's classic novel *Brave New World* is a frightening vision of a society where all individuality has been abolished and where the mantra of the all-controlling state is "Community, Identity, Stability." Here all suffering is relieved through sedative medicine, everything revolves around optimizing consumption, and everybody is predestined for their place in society with no opportunity to influence their own destiny. Such is life under the rule of the ultimate centralized, effective, and bureaucratic state. "The community" is a grey mass of individuals with no autonomous will, a mass of humanity.

Even though today's western societies are still relatively far from Huxley's dystopia, there are elements that one might directly refer to the European welfare states. Great public sectors carry out the tasks expected of them, and in the process they bureaucratize, centralize, and control things they should not. Accordingly, it becomes easy to blame the state for one's problems instead of taking responsibility for the life one wishes to live.

Of the fathers of personalism, Russian philosopher *Nikolai Berdyaev* has dealt most extensively with this problematic. According to Berdyaev, the state is merely a human means, but it often decays and abuses its power to use humans as a means to its own ends. Instead of the state existing for the sake of citizens, citizens start existing for

> **The individual never has to do with another human without holding some of his or her life in his hand. We are each other's world and each other's destiny.**
> Danish philosopher K. E. Løgstrup

the sake of the state. This is caused by, among other things, what one might call the *entropy* of the state. The bigger the state, the more it is bound to grow. Berdyaev believes that all human institutions are in constant danger of error and abuse and that this is mainly because of the process that he calls "objectification."

The human subject sets up concepts, ordinances, and institutions in order to serve human life, but instead these gain a life of their own, become objectivized, and end up demanding that humans submit to them and serve them. The only defense against such tendencies is what Berdyaev calls a personalist *transvalutaion* (re-evaluation) of values: The values of society must be saturated with personalism.

Bureaucracy and centralization are some of the most dangerous latent distortions of the modern state, which is why Berdyaev advocates decentralization and a pluralist society. In a word, the state must constantly be trimmed and kept down. In order for society to develop, it may be necessary that the state briefly assume new tasks and power, but as soon as it is possible, the state should return this power to the persons and communities it concerns.

Deeply seated in the personalist way of thinking is the notion that power should be seated as close to the individual as possible. The further removed and the more centralized power becomes, the poorer become the individual person's conditions for influencing his or her own life. The state should therefore deal only with that which cannot be attended to at a lower level. Personalism thus holds a principle of subsidiarity or proximity which entails that political decisions should be made at the lowest possible political level.

Berdyaev has been called the philosopher of freedom, because he so stresses freedom as the precondition of human development, personality, and creative expression. Humans want freedom and have the capacity for it, but according to Berdyaev, we also fear freedom, because we fear responsibility. There are endless historical examples of people giving up their freedom.

In his central work *Man's Slavery and Freedom*, Berdyaev treats the human disposition for slavery. Humans become slaves to utopias, to society, religions, technology, even to ourselves. Humans have countless ways of making slaves of ourselves, and we are seldom aware of our own enslavement, but according to Berdyaev, freedom is always

NIKOLAI BERDYAEV – FREEDOM FOR COMMUNITY

Nikolai Berdyaev (1874-1948) was born into an aristocratic military family. As early as his adolescent years, he acquainted himself through his father's collection of books with philosophers such as Immanuel Kant, Arthur Schopenhauer, and G. W. F. Hegel and decided upon an academic career.

He enrolled as a student at the University of Kiev in 1894. He was soon attracted to Marxism, and in 1898, he was arrested during a student protest and subsequently expelled from the university. He married in 1904 and moved to Saint Petersburg. There he immersed himself fully in the philosophical and religious debate, gradually reaching a position of his own, for which he became known as a Christian existentialist.

Berdyaev's relatively swift goodbye to Marxism was primarily due to Marxism's materialist anthropology, which he regarded as "two-dimensional." He reacted strongly to any reductionist account of the human person. In his work, he

the precondition for humans to realize our potential, and it takes a heroic struggle to gain that freedom.⁷³

Personalist critique of the system

Ingrained in personalism, then, is a critique of systems, a critical view of the established order. This is true when systems are obviously oppressive, as with communist rule up until the fall of the Berlin Wall. But western societies may also be said, in a more obscure manner, to be ruled by an alienating and, in a sense, totalitarian ideology.

Czech system critic and later-to-be president *Václav Havel* would drew upon a broad spectrum of thinkers: Fyodor Dostoyevsky held the first and the greatest significance for him, but he was later influenced by Friedrich Nietzsche and Lev Tolstoy as well as Max Scheler and Søren Kierkegaard. "My thought has been oriented anthropocentrically, not cosmocentrically," writes Berdyaev in his book *The Russian Idea*, thus pointing to his own fundamental philosophical problem: "the problem of an objectivization which is based upon alienation, the loss of freedom and personality, and subjection to the general and the necessary. My philosophy is decisively personalist and according to the fashionable terminology now established it might be called existential."⁷⁴

In 1922, the Bolshevik regime expelled Berdyaev, Lossky, and 158 other prominent intellectuals from the Soviet Union. They left the country on the so-called *Philosopher's Ship*. Many of them first settled in Berlin, but the economic and political development then forced several of them to move on, mainly to Paris.

Here, Berdyaev gathered a large group of personalists for what became known as *Berdyaev's Sundays*. Thinkers such as Gabriel Marcel, Emmanuel Mounier, Etienne Gilson, Jacques Maritain, and others often met on Sundays in Berdyaev's home.

hardly call himself a personalist, but in several ways, he speaks to a personalist tradition. Two good exaples are his account of the nature of power and the necessity of "counter-power" and his thoughts on "anti-political politics."

Even though Havel primarily wrote and acted against a communist system, he was fully aware that western society was also subject to an alienating ideology. He understood that it makes no great different whether state power or capitalism oppresses people and makes them slaves to an impersonal system. He therefore called for careful consideration and encouraged people no longer to live for our own sake: "It seems to me that if the world is to change for the better it must start

VÁCLAV HAVEL – ANTIPOLITICAL POLITICS

Václac Havel (1936-2011) was a Czech author and one of the main figures behind the fall of communism in Czechoslovakia's "Velvet Revolution" of 1989. After the introduction of democracy, he became president, first of Czechoslovakia and, following the country's division in 1993, of the Czech Republic.

Havel protested against the totalitarian communist state and the ideology that in his opinion enabled this state to continue oppressing its citizens. The ideology made people capable of ignoring the fact that they lived "in the lie." Havel believed that if humans were to live "in the truth," then they had to take responsibility for their own lives and free themselves of the oppressive system by rebelling against it with their actions.

Together with other public intellectuals, he wrote the manifesto *Charta 77*, criticizing among other things the failure of the authorities to recognize basic human rights. The manifesto was banned, and Havel spent several years in pri-

with a change in human consciousness, in the very humanness of modern man. Man must in some way come to his senses. He must extricate himself from this terrible involvement in both the obvious and the hidden mechanisms of totality, from consumption to repression, from advertising to manipulation through television. He must rebel against his role as a helpless cog in the gigantic and enormous machinery hurtling God knows where. He must discover again, within himself, a deeper sense of responsibility toward the world, which means responsibility toward something higher than himself."[75]

Another aspect to which Havel paid grave attention is the fact that power inevitably corrupts, and the more centralized power is, the greason. After the revolution, Havel, who harbored no political ambitions, was elected president. Havel's "unpolitical" understanding of politics focused on respect for the individual:

"I favor "antipolitical politics," that is, politics not as the technology of power and manipulation, of cybernetic rule over humans or as the art of the utilitarian, but politics as one of the ways of seeking and achieving meaningful lives, of protecting them and serving them. I favor politics as practical morality, as service to the truth, as essentially human and humanly measured care for our fellow humans. It is, I presume, an approach which, in this world, is extremely impractical and difficult to apply in daily life. Still, I know no better alternative."[76]

When Havel speaks of politics as "morality put into practice," "a service to truth", and "care for one's neighbor," he speaks directly into a personalist tradition. Politics is not merely a game of power, nor about creating contracts among citizens; rather, the task of organizing communities and giving the people in them the best possible conditions for flourishing is a "service to truth".

Havel does not categorize himself as a personalist, but his thinking is so near to personalism that, together with for instance Jan Patočka (1907-1977), he has been labeled a Prague personalist.[77]

ter the risk and scale of corruption. History has shown that humans have a tendency to dominate others if given the opportunity, which is why power is best situated in the hands of the individual. When humans work cooperatively on projects in communities and institutions, these must be as open, transparent, and accessible as possible. A system with many internal bodies of supervision is a symptom that something is wrong. A system that constantly inspects itself is a sick system bound to keep growing without benefiting the citizens of society.[78]

Critique of capitalism

In the first half of the 20th century, in was clear that personalism shared the social indignation of Marxism at the human cost of capitalism, and

MAX SCHELER – SENSITIVE REASON

Max Scheler (1874-1928) was born in Munich. His mother was Jewish, his Father a protestant, and he himself converted to Catholicism at the age of fourteen. He studied in Munich and Berlin and taught at the universities of Jena and Munich.

Scheler was one of the most colorful of the early phenomenologists, working all his life to develop an ethical personalist philosophy. His main inspiration came from Edmund Husserl (1859-1938), but he also carried on a dialogue with Immanuel Kant (1724-1804), Henri Bergson (1859-1941) and Friedrich Nietzsche (1844-1900). His work has formed part of the foundation for personalist thought, for instance influencing the personalism of Berdyaev in Russia, the dialogical personalists in Germany, and the personalism developed by Wojtyla in Poland.

Scheler's thought focuses on human emotions and human nature. He shows

both philosophies were occupied with human alienation. Mounier was a vehement critic of the way in which capitalism has saturated practically all aspects of human and social life. Capitalism was meant to be a tool under our control, but instead it has become an all-encompassing paradigm for all aspects of life, smothering the spiritual, the personal, and the relational. Capitalism must therefore be shown its proper place in the life of society as well as in personal life.[79]

In his analyses of capitalism, *Max Scheler* believed that he had unmasked it as a cunning, globally growing way of thought, rather than a mere economic system. Economic capitalism, to be sure, has its roots in Protestant ethics, as pointed out by Max Weber. But according to Scheler, the basic way of thinking comes from modern unconscious anxiety, expressing itself in a growing need for (economic) safeguards,

that the ego, reason, and consciousness presuppose a personal sphere – there is no such thing as pure ego, pure reason, or pure consciousness. This implies a critique of the positions of Husserl, Kant, and German idealism. It is the human heart or the seat of love, rather than a transcendent ego, reason, or will, that is the essence of human existence.

Scheler distinguishes amongst various types of emotion, many of which are hidden and personal, but emphasizes love as the core of them all. Drawing upon Blaise Pascal (1623-1662), Scheler argued that humans are fundamentally loving and that love and the emotions have their own logic quite different from the logic of reason.

Scheler thus inscribes himself in the classic and recurring philosophical struggle between "mind and heart," and in stressing the rationality of the emotions, he develops his own type of emotional philosophy. Humans are not characterized by emotions alone, but we experience the world and acquire its values and objectivity through the emotions. This fusion of emotions and reason becomes an important component of personalism.

as well as for personal protection. For Scheler, personalism helps to identify sufficient grounds for condemning this way of thought, namely that capitalism diminishes the value of the individual person.[80] At the same time, personalist critique of capitalism differs notably from that of Marxism. Whereas the Marxist answer, putting it simply, is a material battle of interests ruled by the collective, personalism believes in a struggle of values with the person as its main figure. Whereas Marxism sees alienation in the conditions of *production*, personalism sees it in the conditions of *relationship*, because the realization of the person requires the Other, a fellow human.

Capitalism has developed significantly since the day of Mounier and Scheler, making it hard to imagine that they would have been any less critical today. The tendency of economic thought to eat into one sphere after another and shaping humans in its image has definitely not diminished today.

According to personalism, the ideal conditions would consist in a society where the totality of the community is the living, organic result of each person's free, responsible engagement. In a word: The "we" of human society must never go without the personal "I."

Civil rights

American civil rights proponent *Martin Luther King* took the personalist anthropology as his point of departure. First, he was theoretically interested in personalism, writing his Ph.D. dissertation on personalism at Boston University, and he later backed up his words with action in his activist struggle for the rights of blacks in the US.

King was heavily influenced by the philosophy of natural law, traceable all the way back to Greek philosophy and Aristotle (384-322 BC.) Natural law supposes that humans according to our very nature have our own law and rights. Aristotle distinguished between the specific law that, whether written or unwritten, holds for a par-

PERSONALISM AS OPPOSED TO MARXISM

- Human alienation does not, as claimed by Marxism, occur in relation to an object, but rather a subject. Humans are not alienated from material production, but from human relationships and human community.
- According to personalism, humans are spiritual creatures; religion may therefore be the free breath of humanity and thus not necessarily a sedative opiate.
- Any determinist theory of humanity, evolution, or history belittles the uniqueness and free, creative will of the person and the dynamics of community; the person can never be totalized according to any category.
- Centralization alienates the citizen and robs persons and their communities of initiative, engagement, and responsibility. Power corrupts, and institutions are subject to the law of entropy. The state must therefore perpetually be minimized and only manage what cannot be managed at a lower level: The structures of society are to be subsidized down to the individual.

ticular society, and the universal law that is the law of nature, binding all humans.

This way of thinking was developed further by Thomas Aquinas (1225-1274) who argues that societies should respect the human natural law by striving for *the common good*.[81]

King justified his nonviolent civil disobedience on the basis of this idea that laws may be in accordance with or opposed to natural law, and that natural law is not only universally human, but also universally intelligible.

In his famous letter from the prison in Birmingham, Alabama, where he was held in custody after his arrest during a protest against racial segregation, King responds to the question of how he could encourage breaking the law. The letter illustrates King's own personalism as well as his knowledge of the personalist tradition:

"The answer lies in the fact that there are two types of laws: just and unjust... One has not only a legal but a moral responsibility to obey just laws. Conversely, one has a moral responsibility to disobey unjust laws. I would agree with St. Augustine that 'an unjust law is no law at all.' Any law that degrades human personality is unjust. All segregation statutes are unjust because segregation distorts the soul and damages the personality… Segregation, to use the terminology of the Jewish philosopher Martin Buber, substitutes an 'I-it' relationship for an 'I-thou' relationship and ends up relegating persons to the status of things. Hence segregation is not only politically, economically and sociologically unsound, it is morally wrong and sinful."[82]

MARTIN LUTHER KING – VALUABLE HUMANS

Martin Luther King Jr. (1929-1968) was born into the home of a reverend in Atlanta, Georgia. In 1954, at the age of 25, he became the pastor of a Baptist church in Montgomery, Alabama, and in 1955 he received a Ph.D. in systematic theology from Boston University. In his dissertation he compared the conception of God in the respective works of philosophers and theologians Paul Tillich and Henry Nelson Wieman. In spite of the differences he pointed out in the theology of the two thinkers, King ultimately accused both of holding an impersonal view of God – conceiving of a God with whom a living, prayerful relationship was not possible.[83]

King stood for nonviolent protest, inspired by Gandhi's struggle in India. His work as a civil rights proponent began in Montgomery in 1955, where he headed a mass boycott of the town's buses, prompted by the arrest of Rosa Parks for not giving up her seat for a white man. In 1957 he became the president of the Southern Christian Leadership Conference (SCLC), which worked to equip black churches for nonviolent civil rights protest.

The heyday of King and the civil rights movement was the first half of the

Nonviolent resistance

It is no coincidence that both Martin Luther King in the US and Desmond Tutu in South Africa were proponents of *nonviolent* resistance to the oppressive systems. Causing damage to a human body, and ultimately taking a human life, must be the ultimate violation of that person's worth and rights.

In many ways, violence may be regarded as the antithesis of personalism. Violence is the ultimate depersonalization. Violence is the

---

1960s, when a number of important marches took place. It was on the occasion of the march to Washington D.C. in 1963 that King delivered his famous "I have a dream" speech. Martin Luther King received the Nobel Peace Prize in 1964 for his work against racial discrimination. Over the following years, he carried on his work and became engaged in the resistance against the Vietnam War and against poverty. In 1968 he was shot in Memphis, Tennessee, while visiting the town to support the black sanitation workers in their struggle for higher pay and better work conditions.

King was introduced to personalist thought during his studies at Boston University, which was at the time the stronghold of American personalism[84]. He wrote a dissertation on personalism and subscribed to its thinking: "This personal idealism remains today my basic philosophical position. Personalism's insistence that only personality – finite and infinite – is ultimately real strengthened me in two convictions: it gave me metaphysical and philosophical grounding for the idea of a personal God, and it gave me a metaphysical basis for the dignity and worth of all human personality."[85]

When Martin Luther King held his famous speech, "I have a dream," on August 28, 1963 on the stairs of the Lincoln Memorial in Washington D.C. this was in a fundamental way a personalist dream. It was a dream that had sprouted in his childhood, found its philosophical form at Boston University, and unfolded in the American civil rights movement.

rejection of communion with another – it is the direct destruction of community and relationship. When one human commits violence against another, not only does the victim suffer physical and/or mental injury; the perpetrator too is destroyed, brutalized, dehumanized.

What may be termed organized violence, in warfare, is also problematic for personalism. Soldiers are trained precisely to regard the

BOSTON PERSONALISM

Martin Luther King was heavily influenced by the so-called Boston school of personalists. In the present book we have traced the roots of personalism back several centuries. However, it was in early 20th century North America that a distinct personalist school of philosophy began to emerge. In 1908 professor Borden Parker Bowne (1847-1910) of Boston University published his book *Personalism*.[86] The book presented Bowne's academic efforts to develop and define personalism as a unique and coherent position in modern philosophy. Bowne provided a rigid systematic presentation of the personalist position, and he proceeded to treat all the fundamental theological and philosophical problems from his own personalist vantage point.

Bowne's philosophical conception of the human person was based upon the idea of a coherent, conscious self that was aware of its own existence and capable of autonomous knowledge and action. The latter category, action, was also important for Bowne's philosophy, since he held that the self was not to be thought of in abstract terms, but rather a reality that manifested itself only in the concrete – through human action.

Bowne was a Christian and a former pastor, rooted in the Methodist tradition. His basic philosophy was founded upon theism – the presupposition that there is such a thing as God – and his anthropology started from the notion of humans as created in the image and likeness of God. This fundamental point of departure is very important, because it allowed Bowne to say that perfect personhood is found only in God, and that human selfhood, and thus also personhood, exists

enemy as something other than persons. In order to make a good combat soldier, the innate respect for others must first be broken down.

The enemy must be devalued from being a fellow human with dignity to a worthless opponent. It is no secret how this process of destruction is carried out; through physical and mental pressure, the soldier's ability to make autonomous decisions is broken down, leav-

---

only as an imperfect reflection of divine selfhood. This theistic personalism may be seen as Bowne's reaction against the impersonal naturalist philosophy of his time, not least the work and heritage of Darwinian philosopher and anthropologist Herbert Spencer (1820-1903).

These features were carried over into the next generation of American personalists. The main representatives of this generation were Edgar S. Brightman (1884-1953) and Albert C. Knudson (1873-1953). Brightman defined personalism as "a philosophy which not only holds that God is personal, but also holds that personality is irreducible, ultimate reality; that the impersonal cannot explain the personal; and that everything which we call impersonal, including the very world of physical nature, is nothing but experience or activity of personality."[87] In other words, according to Brightman we humans only know reality in as far as it interacts with us as persons (and originates with God as person). Philosophy, in this personalist perspective, cannot speak for instance of a purely material reality existing independently of personal knowledge or activity. Brightman also emphasizes the fundamentally active character of personhood by saying that impersonal perfection is static whereas personal perfection is dynamic.[88]

Knudson was the great communicator among the early personalists. Apart from striving to provide a systematic yet summary presentation of the personalist philosophy, Knudson was also the first to attempt a historical genealogy of personalism. These two aspects of Knudson's work in combination produced a systematic classification of various branches of personalism, according not least to their various theological foundations.[89]

ing a "good soldier" who will follow orders more or less blindly, regardless of the content of the order in question.

From a personalist point of view, this is a wholly unacceptable procedure. But what alternatives are there? War is so ingrained a part of our way of thinking that most of us cannot imagine a world without war. However, the wars in Iraq and Afghanistan have caused us to fundamentally question the justification of war as an effective solution to problems, reminding the international community of the timeless insights that in war, "truth is the first victim" and, "in war, there are no winners." In spite of this experience, public debate is still shaped by the fact that armed intervention is often suggested as one of the most obvious solutions when new conflicts arise. We have difficulty imagining any other methods – and when other methods are suggested, they are often ridiculed and regarded as naïve.

Even though we live in a world that builds to a great extent on the right of the strongest, the philosophy of nonviolence is still successful. For personalists, the moral grounds are decisive, but there is another good argument: Nonviolence actually turns out to be a very effective weapon, as both Desmond Tutu and Martin Luther King have shown.

In the book *Why Civilian Resistance Works*, Erica Chenoweth and Maria J. Stephan show how, over the period from 1900-2006, campaigns based on nonviolent methods have succeeded in twice as many cases as those resorting to violence. Since 1980, nonviolent movements of resistance have undergone massive growth, whereas armed rebel movements experience declining support. Another of the book's points is that a society where those in power were instituted through a violent revolution will itself be more violent than societies where revolution takes place without violence.[90]

The Arab spring and especially the revolution in Egypt has been characterized by a very conscious philosophy of nonviolence, inspired by people like Gandhi and the American nonviolence guru Gene Sharp, who was once nominated for the Nobel Peace Prize.

During the revolution of January and February 2011, Egyptian protesters were met with curfews, violence, tear gas, and gunfire, but they insisted upon responding through nonviolent protests in which doormen and millionaires, Christians and Muslims, young and old, women and men walked hand in hand. Sharp's central point is precisely that the structures of power ultimately depend upon obedience of subjects towards those in power. If the subjects cease to obey, power vanishes.

Some personalists are pacifists, but not all; and yet personalism is generally characterized by anti-militarism and a willingness to go very far in solving conflicts in a peaceful, diplomatic manner.

Dignity under pressure

Looking from an historical perspective, there has certainly been progress over the centuries, as far as respect for the inherent human dignity is concerned. The UN human rights enactment has definitely had its significance, even if there is a long way to go before human rights are protected in all parts of the world. However, we now have a broadly recognized international standard to measure violations against.

Even so, we may be justly concerned with developments over the past few decades. For instance, a shift seems to have occurred in the general view of the use of torture.[91] Studies suggest that this shift is an effect of 9/11 and the so-called war on terrorism. Respect for the ban on torture has declined, and it is questioned whether the ban should be maintained at all. This shift has not only occurred among politicians, military agents, and decision makers, but also among the population in general.

Furthermore, we see new types of war that are even more depersonalized. The US makes large-scale use of so-called "drones" to liquidate persons regarded as a threat to national security. These people are killed without any sort of public legal process, by "soldiers" located thousands of miles away, controlling planes as in a video game. Killing people thus becomes a sort of virtual battle in which the other's humanity is efficiently pushed away. Also, many civilians become collateral damage, since bombs are still unable to distinguish the alleged bad guys from the innocent.

Protests against the executions of Al Qaeda leader Osama Bin Laden and former Libyan head of state Muammar Gaddafi have been remarkably meek. Many of us shrug, thinking: "Oh well, weren't they asking for it? I can't feel sorry for them…" But what happened to the principle of equal human dignity and the right to fair, public treatment at an independent, impartial court?

In many western countries, leading politicians have argued against granting citizenship to stateless refugees, labeling them a threat to national security. The problem, according to a personalist anthropology, is that the stateless have no official rights and that their inalienable rights as persons are not protected. Such cases are made in spite of the UN convention proclaiming the right to citizenship for the world's twelve million stateless persons.

Likewise, human dignity is under pressure in the sphere of healthcare. Technological advances have made it widely possible to locate and discard unwanted children – because of the risk of a more or less severe handicap, or ultimately because of the child's gender. A current and disturbing example of this development is so-called "abortion tourism," where pregnant women travel to a country where it is possible for them to have an abortion, because they are unhappy with the gender of their child. A shift has occurred in our attitude towards life as such and towards the demands for a "perfect life," free from, for instance, physical and mental disabilities.

The future holds disturbing perspectives that will almost inevitably result in a completely new view of humanity. It will be possible through genetic manipulation to design people with precisely the desired characteristics.

Summary

Personalism stresses the uniqueness and infinite value of the individual human. Humans are inviolable and must not be made subject to any kind of violation. When people and institutions violate persons, they depersonalize them and treat them like things that are of no other value than that which they violently ascribe to them.

Humans have value in and of ourselves, and each human being should therefore be treated respectfully, regardless of ethnicity, culture, religion, and social status.

While humans are unique persons with inviolable dignity, we are bound to and engaged in communities – or brotherhoods. The human commonality (of destiny) means that when one person is oppressed or violated, all of humanity is affected.

Personalism sees it as its task constantly to battle all manner of violations against human dignity and freedom – no matter in whose name the violation is committed, and regardless of whether people, institutions, states, or other systems commit it. It recognizes the need for power to be spread out as much as possible and to become as open and transparent as possible.

Challenges to Personalism
You and I – on Our Way

Personalism gained a prominent position in the early twentieth century, both in the States and in large parts of Europe. Its golden age was the period from the 1930s to the 1960s. However, personalism never gained a strong popular foothold, nor did it become a broad intellectual movement.

Against this background one might ask: If personalism is so outstanding, and if so many intuitively agree with it as soon as it is presented to them, then why is it practically unknown outside academic circles? And why do many societies move away from a personalist practice and become increasingly depersonalized?

Such questions have naturally occupied many personalists, and they have occasionally attempted to answer them.

At a philosophical level, personalism's failure to break through is often explained with reference to the fact that Jean-Paul Sartre's existentialism became so dominant after the Second World War that it either absorbed or eliminated many personalist philosophies. And at a very concrete level, Mounier's early death in 1950 shifted the personalist movement in France and Europe into a lower gear, because of the degree to which he had been its most charismatic and best-known figure. Following Mounier's death, the movement lacked an anchor, and his work was not enough of a foundation since, compared to Sartre's massive oeuvre, it was quite modest in its extent.

One might ask whether personalism might have been more effectively and permanently consolidated if Mounier, besides his activism, among other things as editor of the journal *Esprit*, had taken the time to prepare a more rigid and comprehensive formulation of his thinking.

The answer is that, for Mounier, this would have gone against the very spirit of personalism. He believed that, since "personalism's central affirmation being the existence of free and creative persons, it introduces into the heart of its constructions a principle of unpredictability which excludes any desire for a definitive system."[92] This attitude has kept many of personalism's main figures from cutting across the many branches and posing a singular systematic, canonical presentation of personalism.

Mounier was very conscious of this disposition: "Spare us from the very demand for a definition of personalism. By prematurely marking it with the stamp of clear knowledge, we would turn it into a thing of our own, staged by and for us, whereas we really consider it an unresolved tradition and a future that we are still discovering – that is, in both directions a voyage of discovery, a spiritual current, pregnant with the past and with an uncertain future which will not show its final contours until its promises are fulfilled."[93]

This intention to form a common dynamic and open process of understanding is very appealing, but it has also blurred the main message to some extent.

Personalism has also been accused of not being an original philosophy, since many of its elements are already found in the existing philosophical tradition. This is true in a sense, but this critique pertains to practically all of philosophy, which is, roughly put, merely a set of footnotes to the philosophy of antiquity. All basic philosophical problems have already been touched upon in antique philosophy. The original contribution of personalism, as with other philosophical movements, is to take central elements of earlier thinkers and orchestrate them in such a way as to form a new way of thinking.

> Since personalism's central affirmation being the existence of free and creative persons, it introduces into the heart of its constructions a principle of unpredictability which excludes any desire for a definitive system.
>
> EMMANUEL MOUNIER

Personalism's contribution is the cultivation and new presentation of the concept of personhood, making it the starting point for metaphysics as well as ontology, epistemology, and ethics. Personalism, in other words, is an anthropology that poses the person as the principle for all that is good (ethics), for all that is (ontology), and for how we understand it all (epistemology).

No popular breakthrough

Another explanation for personalism's failure to break through on a broader scale is that is was never popularized. Its staple principles were described in academic discourse and discussed first and foremost behind university walls and in philosophical journals. It is thought-provoking that today it is difficult to find a popular description of the personalist anthropology and way of thought.

This is not to say that no attempts were made to draw political consequences from personalism. For much of the late twentieth century, there were, especially in Germany and France, politicians who found inspiration in personalism, and it gained a footing in the Christian Democrat parties in particular. Not least the *Fathers of Europe* – the politicians who articulated the vision of a united Europe – were influenced by personalism. These figures included Robert Schumann, Konrad Adenuaer, and Alcide de Gasperi, whose primary vision was never to allow a devastating war among European countries to happen again.

Professor Uffe Østergård has made the point that in order to find what is unique to Europe, one should investigate the events in which the European culture has made its quantum leaps and without which Europe and its history would be incomprehensible. Naturally, there are the three classical "events": Jerusalem, Athens, and Rome (Jerusalem: the Judeo-Christian heritage; Athens: philosophy; Rome: organization and state apparatus). To these should be added, according to Uffe Østergaard, two events that have the same significance in the

THE FATHERS OF EUROPE

The politicians who worked towards the foundation of the European Communities, and have set the trend ever since, define themselves as personalists. The Founding Fathers of the European Community, the greatest political movement in Europe, and the first president of the EU come from a personalist background.

When the EU presidential post was first established, Christian Democrat, personalist, and former Belgian prime minister Herman Van Rompuy was appointed the first president. Just a few days after this historical appointment, he laid out his political vision in a speech, "Personalism in political action," in which he unfolded personalism historically, conceptually, and politically.[95]

Likewise, it was personalists who spearheaded the effort to unite Europe around peace, cooperation, and development after the Second World War. At the 1948 congress in the Hague, where the great postwar political and cultural leaders laid the foundations for the cooperation that eventually became the European Council and the EU, personalist Denis de Rougemont was asked to write the draft for a declaration for the Europeans.

"Human dignity is Europe's most noble achievement and freedom its true strength," declared de Rougemont. "Both are at stake in our struggle. The union of our continent is a necessity for the freedom that we have won, but also for the expansion of these goods to all of humankind. The destiny of Europe and world peace depend upon this union."[96]

evolution of the Europe we know today, namely the Age of Enlightenment, and also the development following the Second World War, when the Christian Democrat movement spearheaded the transformation of the personalist tradition into politically operative concepts in Europe.

According to Uffe Østergaard, this effort was just as innovative and carries the same weight as, for instance, the Age of Enlightenment.[94] Human dignity and mutual connectedness, the principle of subsidia-

> A course had thus been set which was to shape the European community for many years to come. In the period since then, personalist politicians, mainly from Christian democrat parties, have also greatly influenced European politics. Main figures such as Robert Schumann, Jean Monnet, Alcide de Gasperi, Konrad Adenauer, Jacques Delors, Herman Van Rompuy, and many others are self-declared personalists. The largest group in the European Parliament is the Christian Democratic EPP who in their official plan of action declare themselves a "personalist movement."
>
> Jacques Delors, socialist and chairman of the European Commission from 1985 to 1995 also expresses his personalist inspiration: "As a personalist, a disciple of Emmanuel Mounier," begins one of Delors' speeches in which he focuses upon the aim of the European community and its efforts to "unite that which to many seems irreconcilable; the emergence of a united Europe and loyalty to one's home country; the need for a European superpower capable of dealing with the problems of our time, and the absolute necessity of preserving our roots in the form of nations and regions; and the decentralization of responsibility so as to never leave to a greater organ what a smaller one would be able to handle better."[97]
>
> It is certainly debatable how well the European community of today reflects these personalist values, but it is an irrefutable fact that the fathers of Europe and the underlying current in the community has been an attempt to put personalism into practice and political action.

rity, and all the other key European concepts may have existed as philosophical/theological concepts for centuries, but it was through the work of personalist politicians that they were made operational and became corner stones of the European community.

In the period that followed the Second World War, the political implementation of personalism thus had some success. But relatively soon a situation arose where it was not so easy to identify personalist elements in the parties that claimed to be built upon it. And one does not immediately think of the EU project as inspired by personalism. Today, the EU is all but entirely known for the exact opposite, for being a centralist project which drowns out the individual.

The fact that today personalism is primarily associated with right-of-center parties can be explained by its being, as it were, locked into the time in which its political application first occurred. It was a time of collectivism, and personalism was shaped in opposition to forms of socialism and communism in which the individual was neglected. Therefore the parties inspired by personalism in Europe naturally found their place on the conservative/liberal wing, in opposition to socialist currents.

And to a great extent they stayed there, even though the times changed and the spirit of the age became ever more individualistic and materialistic. With their bourgeois, liberal profile, the parties inspired by personalism have made only a feeble effort at what today seems the obvious task: speaking out against individualism and market-ruled capitalism. On a broad scale, personalism has therefore been lost in practical politics. Elements of it may be found in various political parties, but it is rarely backed up with personalist arguments.

Resistance to personalism

Personalism's failure to break through on a broad scale has not spared it from being contradicted. In the previous century, when the main currents were totalitarianism and collectivism, personalism was accused of being too individualist. In short, from the perspective of communism and collectivism, personalism is individualistic.

Nowadays the problem is to a great extent the opposite: In a capitalist and individualist society in which human consumption and independence are the dominant values, personalism becomes a thorn in the flesh because it is critical of that which isolates people from the community – because it speaks out against turning humans into customers or consumers instead of persons. In other words: In the eyes of liberalism and individualism, personalism is too collectivistic. Another strand of critique against personalism has held that its strong emphasis upon the unique, inviolable, and absolute value of the person leaves an opening for the exploitation and, ultimately, the destruction of the environment and of nature's resources. This is a fully legitimate question to raise, since for personalism, the human person's value is incomparably the greatest. Hence, personalists and politicians founded in personalism have reacted against all attempts to place human value alongside that of animals and nature as such.

In practical terms, however, this principle does not cause personalism to regard the value of nature as reducible to being of service to humans. This is because personalism has to a great extent developed within theistic settings, marked by the view that however special the value of the human person, a creator God has also created and willed nature and the animals, thus endowing them with an independent value of their own. Human worth is absolute and inviolable, but humans have a task of responsible stewardship.

Furthermore, it has become clear in our time that responsible conduct towards nature is a necessity, not just for the sake of nature itself, but also for the sake of our fellow humans. What is good for nature and the environment is good for humanity as well. If we prey upon nature and create imbalances within it, more often than not the most vulnerable humans are the first to suffer.

A threat to those in power

Another element to explain why personalism never caught on might be that in its struggle against human depersonalization through systems and institutions, personalism is very radical; and the sweeping changes it implies would seem to pose a threat not least to those in power. It asks some of the questions that we in the western world would rather forget about.

According to researcher Rachel Metheny, that we live in an inhuman and depersonalized world is illustrated by state-sanctioned killing in the world's most powerful country – the United States of America – as well as by the fact that world poverty could be overcome with a minimum of the wealth of the West. Metheny claims that this situation is compromised by the ethics and demands of personalism, making personalism, in other words, a hassle.[98] For instance, given that the U.S. have spent more than three billion dollars on waging war in Iraq, it is difficult to answer the question of whether this was really the right way to manage the nation's economy.

One counter move has thus been to characterize personalism as naïve. This strategy is practically seen on a daily basis in political debate – not aimed at personalism in particular, but generally against views that question the status quo. "We cannot save the entire world," is a typical argument against raising the amount spent on foreign aid or against a proposition to receive a larger share of the UN refugee quota. Apart from the impertinence of the argument – nobody argues that any country is supposed to save the entire world – it also completely misses the mark according to personalist ethics.

First of all, speaking of "the whole world" amounts to a depersonalization of the human person, since those we are to help are humans who should be met as persons. And no, nobody can save everybody, but saving as many as possible has infinite value; because every single person is infinitely valuable.

> In the future, we shall see the first stirrings of an understanding that we cannot be content to tend to our own interests, but that as citizens of the world we have some common challenges on a global scale to solve.
>
> Sociologist Emilia van Hauen

Second, we should not underestimate what one person or just a few people are capable of achieving. When Rosa Parks refused to give up her seat to a white man on a local bus in Montgomery on December 1, 1955, it became the starting point for the first campaign of the American civil rights movement; and it became an important symbol for the entire movement.

The human potential

Personalism is a positive anthropology in the sense that personalists think highly of the human potential. To be sure, humans are far from perfect, and we have a tendency to oppress others or let ourselves be oppressed. But when humans have the opportunity to realize ourselves in freedom and in relationship with others, we are capable of great deeds.

Personalism, then, is far from a pessimistic anthropology, which might claim that humans will always act according to our own selfish interests; an anthropology that easily develops into the view – some would say the cynical and comfortable view – that it is not possible to change the world, since we humans are the way we are, end of story.

Personalists are attracted to the dream of a better world. The most important tools are the struggle against depersonalization and alienation, as well as the personalization of society in so far as this is possible (i.e. to bring persons, dignity, engagement, and relationships into play). A new imagination is needed in which people think "out of the box" and imagine how things might be. Just like the dissidents in Eastern Europe imagined living in freedom without an oppressive communist system. Just like the black Americans who did not give up, but fought against racial segregation. Or like the South Africans who imagined a South Africa with no apartheid. How many contemporaries actually believed that these projects were realistic? And yet, in each case it turned out to be possible.

Personalism would claim that the problem for us humans is that we too easily let ourselves be limited by systems and structures. That we become the servants of systems that become ends in themselves instead of being the ones who control these systems. Resignation – and with it passivity – is thus the great temptation for the personalist, a temptation that people must help each other to resist. The system and those in power attempt to buy citizens into silence, be it with religion or with flat screen television sets.

The entropy of the system

Why do we allow our society to move away from a personalist practice and become ever more depersonalized?

Part of the explanation is the tremendous difficulty of counteracting what personalists call the entropy of the system. All things being equal, any system will fight not only to maintain itself, but also to expand itself. In practice it often happens that systems and institutions grow compulsively.

An active and conscious resistance is therefore required – and it will often be a difficult struggle. This is not only because the systems against which one struggles are often strong, but also because there are typically a number of good arguments in favor of the system.

Furthermore, it can be difficult to distinguish what is for the good of the system from what is for the good of humans. One good example is freedom of choice, which has been sold to the citizens of the western world as a surpassing good. But as demonstrated by Danish debater Rune Lykkeberg, freedom of choice exists not so much for the sake of citizens as for the sake of the system.

"It is about making the systems work better: If institutions experience citizens as critical users, they are forced to deliver their best.... By thus demanding free choice, one puts the system before citizens – citizens are given formal options that are of use only to a few, but which may be used against them, as all systems are aware."[99]

One might argue that a more efficient system is in the interest of citizens. But is freedom of choice necessarily an unconditional good? Not according to studies in happiness. Too much freedom of choice can easily result in poorer quality of life, since it is stressful for people constantly to have to make important choices with consequences that are hard to assess.[100] In this instance too, one ends up with an economic argument: free choice is good because it makes products cheaper.

A society of indoctrination

When asked what is most important in life, by far the majority of people in the western world would reply: family, relationships, love etc. Most of us know quite well what makes us happy. It is not the consumption of material things.

The interesting thing is that many of us act in direct contradiction of our knowledge. Even though we know what is best for us and what makes us happy, our priorities do not correspond to our knowledge. For instance, we organize ourselves in a manner that makes it difficult for us to take care of our next of kin.

Lise Andersen, business economist and psychology graduate puts it as follows: "I have to work more so that we can afford to have others look after my children and my old mother. Since I don't have the time myself. But my mother won't be particularly happy with being cared for by others. She would be happier if it were me who would come more often and help her. And I would be happier if I were able to help her. Studies tell us that we become happier by giving to others. Still, we have organized ourselves so that we work ourselves halfway to death in order to pay others to do what we'd be better off doing ourselves."[101]

Why is it like this? One reason is that we live in a society that constantly bombards us with the message that more consumption will make us happy. In recent years, commercialization has spread with such lack of restraint that one can no longer even be sure that schoolbooks in Europe are exempt from advertising, and even public companies and institutions now allow space for private advertising.

It is naïve to imagine that this commercialization will not have its intended effect. It is very difficult to uphold one's belief that it is not material acquisitions that make me happy, for the simple reason that I am constantly told the opposite.

Another explanation for why we act contrary to our own interests is that even though we want freedom and have the capacity for it, we also fear it, because we fear responsibility. According to personalist philosopher Berdyaev, humans have a tendency to become slaves to utopias, society, technologies, and even to ourselves. Humans have countless ways of letting ourselves be enslaved, and we are seldom aware of our slavery.[102]

In other words, we are ever so easily entrapped by the systems and institutions that surround us. Upholding one's freedom by, for instance, prioritizing the intimate relationships in one's life therefore requires putting up a fight. What we intuitively perceive as right is not necessarily the easiest way.

> **The insight that we become human through others is clearer to people today. Charity is not merely an abstract concept, but rather it has become something alive and concrete in many people's lives.**
>
> Danish debater Knud Aarup

The time for counteraction has come

However, there are many signs that a broad reaction is taking place. Whether to call it personalism or not is irrelevant in this context. Ever more people experience the emptiness of materialism and begin to make relationships their priority by, for instance, getting involved in volunteer work for others.

Danish sociologist Emilia van Hauen speaks of a paradigm shift: "In the future, we shall see the first stirrings of an understanding that we cannot be content to tend to our own interests, but that as citizens of the world we have some common challenges on a global scale to solve. This will require us to independently take responsibility at both the individual and the organizational level for behaving in a manner that benefits the whole, and also at times to set aside what is to our own advantage in order to create a more sustainable world in the long run."[103]

Public manager and debater Knud Aarup also speaks of a paradigm shift that he calls a moral and ethical one. He believes that we today take our neighbor into account as part of our personal sphere of responsibility, far more than we used to: "The insight that we become human through others is clearer to people today. Charity is not merely an abstract concept, but rather it has become something alive and concrete in many people's lives."[104]

On the one hand, then, we have moral objections to a lifestyle of private, indiscriminate consumption at the cost of civil society and its virtues. However, another relevant tendency is the so-called "de-growth" movement, traceable at least back to the *Club of Rome* think tank and its 1972 report *The Limits to Growth*. As Serge Latouche, professor of economics at Paris-Sud 11 University has noted, degrowth is not a concept or an overall theory. "Degrowth is just a term created by radical critics of growth theory to free everybody from the economic correctness that prevents us from proposing alternative projects for post-development politics."[105] Degrowth thinkers and activists generally attempt to show, through an economic approach, how the dogma of growth actually lies at the root of many problems that we so eagerly strive to solve though economic growth.

As far as the current economic recession is concerned, degrowth economists challenge the notion that this crisis is merely a tunnel to make our way through to another period of prosperity and reckless consumption. Instead, degrowth is concerned with the greater change that may occur if we rid ourselves of the limited mindset which we have learned from mainstream growth-oriented economics.

Yes, greater change is coming. Not only negative change resulting from an economic crisis, but also a change of mentality, a becoming aware that together we are capable of something. It is a sober assessment of what is fundamentally valuable and actually serves the lives of human beings. Positive initiatives are multiplying, initiatives that counter the depersonalization of our society. We need to support such initiatives, both by making them part of the political order of business, by engaging with them, and by spreading the word and thus passing on inspiration to others.

No matter what we do, we are part of a changing society, and with our choices, great and small, we may contribute to shaping the development. In a personalist direction too, if this is the kind of society we sympathize with and long for. We need not resign ourselves to fate; we can work for the strengthening of positive relationships among engaged and infinitely valuable persons, both in our immediate surroundings and in society at large.

THE ROOTS OF PERSONALISM

The story of personalism is the story of how the human person has been defined throughout history.

The roots of personalist philosophy go as far back as antiquity. Broadly speaking we may say that the foundation of personalism, the concept of the person, was developed in the confrontation between Greek philosophy and the new Christian way of thought in the first few centuries after Christ.

As is so often the case, the concept of personhood is indebted to *Aristotle*. Aristotle asserted that humans are the only beings characterized by reason, *logos*. Animals are otherwise identical to humans, but they are *áloga*, without reason.

The word "person" is used by *Tertullian* (155-230) in discussing the doctrine of the Trinity, and it would soon play a major part in the Church's development of the doctrine of Christ and the conception of the Trinity in the 3rd and 4th centuries.

It also influenced thought concerning the human person. Theologians held that since humans are created in the image of God, the individual human must also be conceived of as reflecting the personal traits of God – or at least having the potential to do so – to develop personality.

In Roman law the concept of personhood became a special category in the essential distinction between a person and a thing. The introduction of the concept occurred simultaneously with changes to Roman culture and increased freedom in society. Anyone who could show up in court was a person, which had consequences for their overall status.

Once Roman law attained personal structure, all humans were regarded as free, except for slaves. A free man was a person and had personality. As a natural consequence, a moral dimension arose; every person was also independent, autonomous, and responsible. Later developments have added a psychological dimension: the person is the mature human being.

Austria's king *Theoderic* (454-526) assigned to the philosopher *Boethius* (480-525) the task of defining what a human being is. He arrived at the conclusion that: "Persona est rationalis naturae individua substantia" – a person is an individual substance of a rational nature. This definition was to have great influence upon all future discussion of the nature of the human person.

The first historical occurrence of the concept of personalism is found in German philosopher and theologian *Friedrich Schleiermacher* (1768-1834), who in 1799 used the term *Personalismus* in his book *Reden über die Religion*. He stressed the importance of that which is actively personal, including the religious feeling.

In the nineteenth and twentieth centuries, personalist schools were formed in various countries. Russia, France, Germany, Poland, and the US are countries with a strong personalist tradition, developing personalist philosophy in cooperation with, as well as over against, other worldviews and anthropologies such as socialism and liberalism.

Postscript
Psychology and personalism

The initial five chapters of this book have introduced personalism and applied it with regard to current challenges. We have traced lines backwards in intellectual history—and outwards into society.

This postscript will depart from the same personalist perspectives, only now relating them to the human being as conceived by psychology. However, we immediately come upon certain interdisciplinary obstacles that arise as we put two different traditions into perspective. As will become clear, the DNA of psychology is inherently individualistic, and while it readily prescribes methods and means, it does not tend to pose values and ends. In addition, many varieties of psychology work from the presupposition that the answers to challenges great and small are to be found in the individual psyche.

A need thus becomes apparent for a psychology founded in relationships and values, and we wish to unfold this project in relation to the personalist view of humans. The postscript should not be perceived as an exhaustive description of a relational psychology. Rather, it should be read as a set of scientifically founded meditations that reflect our journey towards a description of psychological perspectives founded in relationships and values.

Obstacle one: The individualistic roots of psychology

When searching for a definition of psychology, one is referred to the two Greek words psuché (soul) and logía (speech or doctrine of). Originally, psychology is thus defined as "theory of the soul". This definition stems from Greek antiquity, with the philosopher Aristotle (384-322 BC) authoring the first psychology (Jacobsen 2008). Psychology, then, has the soul as its original object of enquiry.

In practice, this field of enquiry entails that the relevant cultural and religious conceptions of the soul have great consequences for the way psychology is framed. The soul is a particularly complex concept, since it is intertwined with matters religious, existential, biological, and philosophical.

Our view of the mental or psychological functions in humans tend to progress in tandem with technological developments. The anthropology of the first half of the twentieth century thus bore the markings of mechanical industrialism, whereas the approach of the twenty-first century saw an anthropology influenced by computer and information technologies. During this period, the mind was viewed as an autonomous and self-governing system that actively processed meaning. This tendency was coupled with a materialization of human mental processes that had previously been shrouded in mystery and incomprehensibility (Nielsen, K. og Tanggaard, L. 2011).

Such an IT-based view of the mind still shapes the anthropology of contemporary psychology. Cognitive psychology, which focuses upon mental processes as the cause of—and the potential sphere of treatment for—psychological ailments, plays a particularly dominant role in the theory and practice of Western psychology.

Analysis and treatment of mental processes tend overwhelmingly to proceed from an individualistic conception of personhood and development. One also finds such an individualistic approach in developmental psychology and classical psychoanalysis. The individualist anthropology of developmental psychology is built partially around Swiss psychologist Jean Piaget's (1896-1980) theories of development, in which human development is viewed as proceeding through biologically conditioned and universal stages (Berk 2003). We likewise encounter the individualist anthropology in classical psychoanalysis, with British psychoanalyst Donald W. Winnicot (1896-1971) representing an essentialist conception of the self as a unique inner core, given prior to the human person's encounter with the world (Jørgensen 2002).

As a whole, psychology finds itself in a situation where human development is viewed, for various reasons, in a thoroughly individualistic light, with an emphasis on mental processes.

British sociologist Nikolas Rose (1947-) describes psychology as an individualizing science that has staged humans as individuals with profound inner psychological depths, offering a linguistic frame of psychological concepts through which one may, as an individual, understand oneself and one's own behavior. Rose observes that the human being has become individualized and psychologized in a manner that functions as constitutive of our being (Rose 1998).

The practical consequence of this anthropological tendency is that the vast majority of human and relational problems are understood as stemming from inner mental disturbances or ailments of the individual mind—matters to be diagnosed and subsequently treated with medicine and/or individual therapy.

Obstacle two: A science without values

In exploring the compatibility of psychology with personalist principles, we soon come upon another obstacle. As we attempt to compare personalistic values with those of psychology, we soon discover that psychology—when practiced within the framework of the natural sciences—holds no inherent values or ends. To be sure, psychology deals extensively with how best to relieve mental ailments, yet it refrains from addressing the possible purpose of suffering and the question of values concerning "the good life in common".

The cause of this lack of values is obvious: In the laborious struggle of psychology to be perceived as a legitimate scientific discipline—a struggle that is to expected as one attempts to place "the soul in the laboratory"—it has been crucial to construct an unambiguously scientific profile—and thus an attempted objectivity—free from the bias of inherent values (Hastrup, K 2006).

J. F. Herbart (1776-1841), the German often credited with founding the discipline of pedagogics, points precisely to the value-neutral status of psychology as justifying the existence of pedagogics:

"Pedagogics as a science depends upon practical philosophy (i.e. ethics) and psychology. The former points out the ends of education and formation, the latter shows us the way, the means, and the obstacles." (quoted in Sprogøe, J. 2008)

Herbert here makes an important point concerning the traditional conception of psychology, namely that it is capable of investigating and stating regularities and connections within the sphere of the human mind, but that it holds no inherent orientation nor values, and thus no answers to existential questions.

This does not mean that psychology becomes "without value" in the sense of being useless or representing no use value. What it means is that psychology—when brought into the field of the natural sciences, where life is regarded as merely an organic process—cannot assign goals, but merely provide a list of methods, supposed connections, and obstacles concerning goals and values that have already been posed.

According to personalism, the allocation of psychology among the natural sciences may lead to the depersonalization of the human being, since the overall view and understanding of humans are reduced according to the materialist ontology of the natural sciences, treating humans as a calculable matter of chemistry and physics. When viewed one-sidedly through the lens of the natural sciences, and when described exclusively with their vocabulary, the human being loses its unique inscrutability and diversity—and science loses its humility. The psychologist becomes a diagnostic expert, capable of exhaustively conceptualizing the mental, chemical processes of the physical human. When a single scientific discourse claims to fully conceptualize the human being, this, according to personalism, amounts to a violation, since the unique personality and dignity of a human can never be calculated nor expressed as a formula.

Obstacle three: Existential answers are not found in the individual

Earlier in history, problems were interpreted and solutions attempted within a theological frame of mind. One would turn to God and the Church whenever one's conditions of life grew serious, painful, and existential. The priest was the figure in power and the mediating agent when it came to understanding God's intention behind life's pain and suffering.

In Greek antiquity as well as in Christianity, two traditions that together have founded our thinking about the soul, a vertical connection or striving towards the divine exists within the soul. Both traditions portray a polarity between the divine "celestial" realm and the terrestrial world of humans. The soul wishes to achieve a connection with its original home, to create unity and harmony. An act that may entail change and transformation (Haaning, A. 2003).

Today we have—in many ways—cut the soul loose from "the higher layers". Surveys have shown that religious beliefs among Danes have suffered no reduction over the past 30-40 years, but that such beliefs have changed in quality. Faith has been individualized—thus becoming a personal and private matter, rarely practiced in community.

This is seen especially in the passage from a common religious belief from which the individual and the community would draw their values in life, towards an individualized spiritual faith from which each person independently derives individualistic values (Andersen and Lüchau 2011).

Simultaneously, vertical ties between the individual and the authorities of family, profession, age groups, tradition, and society, have been drastically reduced. Modern humans have emancipated themselves from arch-authorities and traditional roots, writes Danish historian Henrik Jensen (2006) in his book The Fatherless Society. He explains how an era of vertical orientation has been supplanted by strong criticism of authorities, of the vertical.

The loss of vertical ties corresponds to the loss of an ethics conceived as capable of presentation independently of the individual's emotions. Scottish moral philosopher Alasdair Macintyre describes how humans of late modernity express a characteristic emotivism in which individual emotional reactions become the crucial criterion of right and wrong. We thereby end up with a situation in which it is fundamentally impossible to objectively distinguish right from wrong. The practical implication of this emotivism is that individual emotions weigh heavier than moral requirements or responsibilities (Jørgensen 2002).

One might say that we have lost the vertical ties that brought us a sense of identity as well as self-knowledge, ethics, and a sense of direction in the life of an individual. The individual now stands alone—searching for answers within his or her own soul. This is where psychology plays the important part of interpreting the language of the soul apart from religious, ideological, or political (vertical) ties. Psychology has become the frame of interpretation for all manner of human and existential phenomena, and the concepts and diagnoses of psychology have become common property (Rose 1998)

A fact of which few "explorers of the soul" are aware is that although psychology possesses an outstanding methodological and conceptual apparatus, traditional psychology holds no values for the individual. It does not concern itself with the ethical tenability of engaging in a life journey centered around the ego, with whether effectivity and mental optimization are desirable qualities, nor with the value status of placing small children in institutions forty hours per week.

"What do you feel is right?", asks psychology instead, professionally displaying an objectivity that cannot determine which path is right "for you".

One might say that overall developments have brought with them opportunities for emancipation—from religious obligations as well as from the expectations of family and from the toil of labor. But the experience of obligation has not receded—it has merely been displaced. From duty to God and one's neighbor. To the duties of self-realization, self-optimization, and self-development. Of finding one's own uniquely personal path, guided by the soul's responses, counselled by the methods of psychology, and independently of the opinions of others.

However, this inward search into one's own mind and gut feelings, often assisted by self-help literature, for answers to the great questions of life, often misses the mark.

This being said, It is obviously not the case that the body and the mind have nothing good to tell us. Our stomach tells us quite clearly when we are hungry, our eyes let us know when we are tired—and our anger correspondingly testifies to the experience of unfairness, just as sadness shows how crucial love is. Our bodies, emotions, and mental states hold much valuable information, but feelings cannot be consulted like some superhuman guru with access to the deeper meaning of life and knowledge of future possibilities.

A quick overall glance at society clearly reveals that this project is broken. More people than ever suffer from psychological ailments and are unable to handle the realities of the job market. Many fall victim to self-inflicted harm, eating disorders, anxiety, depression, and stress, and the economy cannot withstand the pressure of caring for—and protecting—these victims.

We have lost our vertical ties—and simultaneously our horizontal ones—to communities. The introverted project of self-development has distanced each one of us from others. As Polish sociologist Zygmunt Bauman (1925-) has said, these postmodern life strategies entail the fragmentation of human relations and a distance from others, who in turn become the objects of aesthetic rather than moral evaluation (Frello 2012).

The individualization of psychology—coupled with the loss of vertical ties—has caused profound loneliness and impotence. Individuals discover that their lack of connections means losing the very identity and self-understanding that grows from encountering the other. Which means losing oneself.

Professor of psychology Carsten René Jørgensen sums up the situation quite concisely:

"Psychologization, emotionalization, and the perpetual quest for authenticity are symptoms of a novel introversion, with the isolated individual seeking an inner homestead after the collapse of the great narratives and the widespread disillusion concerning the possibility of building a sustainable community. Sincerity, emotions, and authenticity become the compass for navigating a fragmented, chaotic world prone to constant change." (2002, 120)

Solution: A psychology of relational values and relational answers

A reinterpretation of psychology is called for. Psychology holds incredible potential for explaining phenomena and prescribing meaningful directions, if it is brought into a context of courage to take a stand concerning the meaningful common life. A context in which deliberation concerning values and ethics is viewed as an obligation rather than a symptom of defective objectivity and professionality in psychology.

It therefore makes sense for us to describe a psychology founded in a relational conception of development and a personalist set of values.

Simultaneously, we can already claim to be clearly distinguishable from traditional psychological relativity and value-neutral objectivity:
- We present a value-driven psychology
- We believe that there are certain natural regularities that govern the good life – regularities that transcend individual emotions and experiences.
- We believe that community must be founded upon explicit ethical goals that serve as points of navigation and supply the individual course of life with direction.
- We found these perspectives in a relational anthropology.

The relational human

One of the most extensive psychological studies in history has surveyed the lives of 724 Americans over the course of 75 years in order to discover the recipe for "the good life." The study was conducted by the Harvard Medical School, starting in 1938 with the selection of 724 teenage boys, half of which were about to begin medical training at Harvard, whereas the other half came from a poor Boston slum. At the beginning of the study, the boys were asked how they could achieve a happy life. A large portion answered that wealth and fame would lead to a happy life—a response reproduced by most people when they are asked the same question today. However, they could not have been more wrong.

The study clearly shows that the recipe for a long and happy life unambiguously consists of good relationships. Head of project Robert Waldinger resolutely notes that "Good relationships keep us happier and healthier (…), and that loneliness kills", and the reason is that loneliness is toxic. Humans that live in isolation from others are less happy, and their overall health and brain functions decline earlier. In addition, these people live shorter lives (Waldinger 2016).

What is the background for characterizing humans as relational? Why are relationships crucial for mental as well as bodily health and well-being?

The relational brain

One of things that indicate most clearly the relational foundation of human existence is the protracted developmental process of the human brain. When comparing humans with animal offspring, we find significant differences in inherent—and early—capabilities. Many have been surprised to see how quickly after its birth a calf or foal will get up and stagger about on its shaky limbs. After a few years, the young gain complete independence and are themselves ready to reproduce.

The development of a human child differs significantly from that of animals. Humans are utterly helpless for many months, they are able to walk unaided only after approximately one year, and they can manage independently only after years of nursing, care, and rearing.

This pronounced difference is due to divergent states of development in the brain at birth. Whereas the animal brain is almost fully developed at birth, this is far from the case with the human brain. Even though the undeveloped state of the newborn's brain carries an enormous cost in the shape of years of helplessness and an enormous task of nursing and care for parents, it simultaneously bestows upon humans an amazing flexibility. The protracted process of development entails that the individual human may acquire the specific language, culture, and set of social and cognitive skills required by the unique community into which it is born. (Harris & Westermann 2015).

Humans thus have an almost infinite—and flexible—potential for development, which provides it with amazing opportunities while simultaneously making it incredibly vulnerable. A brain with virtually infinite possibilities of development also risks not developing at all.

Neurons—a web of open possibilities

If we look at human development from a neurological perspective, research shows that the brain possesses a vast number of neurons at the time of birth. These cells function according to the principle of "USE IT OR LOSE IT", which basically means that a process of trimming takes place in accordance with the individual sequence of experiences. The neurons that find use are gathered into specialized circuits, whereas those that do not are deactivated (Hart 2008).

Early relational experiences thus lay the foundation for the brain's manner of organizing emotional and social processes throughout its life (Hart & Møller 2001). This manner of functioning opens a vast set of possibilities, since the interaction with others tends to strengthen the neurons required for the specific cultural skills expected of the individual.

Correspondingly, a brain subjected to very little interactional experience will shut down a great number of neurons, and—in the worst cases—its neurological structures are irreparably damaged. Sadly, the reality of, for instance, Romanian orphanages has shown that children deprived of stimulating interaction end up with heavily underdeveloped brains, and that some lose the capability of ever learning to communicate linguistically (Hart 2008).

In this sense, it is true to say that one must live in community with humans in order to develop human qualities of one's own. At birth, the brain is not merely a biological organ, but also a social one, developed and organized through empathic contact. Even though early experience influences the neurological organization of the brain more permanently, the brain does continue to transform itself throughout life (Hart 2008). Human biology and mentality continue to depend upon—and to be shaped by—concrete coexistence with other humans.

Identity – a relational process

As already described, modern Western culture is engrossed with an ideology of self-realization in which the goal is to become a more "authentic version of oneself". In light of the described neurological development process, the notion of becoming "oneself" in isolation seems absurd. Without relational interaction, humans undergo no developmental experiences, and the only "self" that is then formed is an underdeveloped one without any finer shades of perspective and with weak social skills.

Naturally, it may be healthy and necessary to spend time alone, but isolated self-discovery and introspection do not serve as a viable path to "finding one's true self". The brain may actually undergo neurological extinction when in a state of loneliness, which may serve to explain the correlation of loneliness with depression and Alzheimer's disease (Richter 2011).

The development of a sense of self and the experience of identity are brought about especially through community with others. The word "identity" means accordance or agreement and comes from the Latin "idem", which means "the same". In order to determine the degree of agreement, one must compare similarities and differences. Through such comparison, an identification and a delimitation take form and thereby become increasingly more refined and nuanced as more opportunities for "relational comparison" arise (Jørgensen 2008).

When encountering another human, one must inevitably identify with one's own personal qualities. Generally speaking, the encounter with another is the very condition of knowing anything at all about oneself. We see and evaluate our own qualities in relation to the qualities we find in others. Encountering others therefore influences our self-perception, as we see in the following—somewhat caricatured—quote:

"Dear Lord, if you can't make me skinny, please make my friends fat." (Unknown)

The very establishment of our identities may be described as a collective process (Gergen 2006). The manner in which one is met or received by other will, over time, become internalized as one's own self-experience or identity. A person who is treated with indifference over an extended period of time will soon begin to experience herself as unimportant. A person, on the other hand, who is treated as valuable will soon perceive himself as valuable.

Relationships – for better or worse

Coexistence seems to be a human condition. We cannot be human without relationships, and our connection to our surroundings is thus an inevitable fact of nature. But coexistence is simultaneously a human possibility. We have options when acting within any given situation. Whether to act in accordance with moral and social rules of play or whether to break them and act in an anti-social and dehumanizing manner (Berthelsen 2004).

Human participation may thus unfold in various directions. We can engage actively within relationships, against relationships, or away from relationships. Within seconds of its birth, the infant actively seeks its first relationships—and this profound, instinctive relational commitment, the inevitable bonding with one's social surroundings, continues to direct a person's path through life.

Relationships can be as amazing, thrilling, and life-giving as they can be brutal, explosive, and destructive. Relationships open and close the doors of destiny, "so that it is simply up to the individual whether or not the other's life will turn out well" (Løgstrup 2010).

Relationships in consumer society

"If someone makes you miserable more than they make you happy, let them go..." (Unknown)

"Don't waste your valuable time with people that are not adding to your growth. Your destiny is too important." (Joel Osteen, American preacher and author).

These quotes express an attitude to relationships typical of our time, evaluating them in instrumental terms: "Does this relationship yield more than it costs me?" "Does this relationship support or impair my personal development?"

There is a strong tendency in society to instrumentalize and dehumanize relationships. A tendency caused by several—related—factors:
- The powerful and instinctive human drive towards what is pleasant and easy.
- Social legitimation of an egocentric focus.
- The widespread illusion of interpersonal independence.

The pursuit of pleasure

Consumer analysts have pointed out that consumption in the modern Western world is motivated by pleasure (Analysis, Nordic Council 2001). The advertising industry deliberately addresses the instinctive needs for pleasure that play such a powerful and dominant part in human behavior. Neurologists actually describe the need for pleasure as the single strongest drive in human life (Kringelbach 2008). We instinctively seek immediate sensations of pleasure, we seek to minimize effort, and we avoid discomfort.

Our longing for pleasure has also infected our interpersonal relationships, which are handled and administered according to their quality of pleasure or experience. Within the field of "experience economics", an experience is divided into four domains that are all significant for its quality. These domains are entertainment, learning, aesthetics, and escapism (Pine & Gilmore 1999).

Quite often, these are the exact factors that we end up associating with a "good relationship", which is expressed in the following questions that typically inform the analysis in popular media of a relationship and its qualities:
- Do you have fun with the person? (Entertainment)
- Can the person challenge you? (Learning)
- Are you attracted to the person's appearance? (Aesthetics)
- Can the person make you "forget about place and time"? (Escapism)

The current instrumental and experience-focused norm for measuring "relational quality" creates a harsh environment for long-term, committed, stimulating relationships of family, friendship, and in broader forms of binding community. We see a drastic increase in the number of lonely people and painful relational breaks.

The social legitimacy of "relational consumption"

The human drive towards pleasure, ease, and minimal effort is no new phenomenon. On the contrary, it is a basic human tendency that serves purposes of survival. The aspects of our existence associated with pleasure, such as food, sleep, social contact, and sex are the very same that ensure our survival—and that of the species. We are utterly dependent upon the ability to feel—and be motivated by—pleasure, which is why the inability to feel pleasure, anhedonia, is associated with depression, schizophrenia, and various forms of substance abuse (Kringelbach 2008).

The legitimacy of pleasure, however, has undergone drastic change over time. During some periods, religious perspectives have idealized asceticism whilst regarding pleasure as a sinful, carnal phenomenon to be restricted as much as possible. Today we see a completely different perspective in which pleasure is legitimated by society—not merely as a permitted activity, but as an actual moral duty of the modern individual (Ugilt 2015).

Slovenian philosopher Alenka Zupančič (2008, 5) describes how being healthy and happy seems to be the current moral imperative and definition of a "good human being":

> "Negativity, lack, dissatisfaction, unhappiness, are perceived more and more as moral faults— worse, as a corruption at the level of our very being or bare life. There is a spectacular rise of what we might call a bio-morality (as well as morality of feelings and emotions), which promotes the following fundamental axiom: a person who feels good (and is happy) is a good person; a person who feels bad is a bad person."

This moral duty to be healthy and happy means that today it is regarded as "morally wrong" to waste one's time being unhappy, working the wrong job, or being married to the wrong person. There is a strong implicit connection between what is moral and what is pleasurable—what feels right to the individual.

Within the individualistic competition state, every person has not only the opportunity, but also the obligation to be happy. And should you fail to facilitate your own happiness, you should feel guilty.

These aspects are a challenge to the establishment of strong relationships and communities. When the urge to choose a relationship based solely upon its potential for pleasure and its quality as an experience wins, we will experience a society that increasingly accepts, legitimates, and actually strengthens the tendencies of depersonalization and dehumanization. In other words, it becomes "politically correct" to consume relationships for one's own good.

The illusion of relational independence

This pervasive focus upon individual actualization and self-improvement seldom expresses a consciously negative intent with regard to the individual's fellow human beings. Few people would say that they feel indifferent about the well-being and personal development of others. The widespread self-oriented attitude rather stems from the prevalent notion that one can—and ought to—live one's life independently of the views and opinions of others. That it is possible to act independently in a world of independent individuals. And correspondingly, that expressing dependence, e.g. concern with someone else's opinion, is weak and something to be ashamed of (Bech 2014).

Numerous recent books describe ways to achieve higher self-esteem—independently of other people. One example is found in the book: "The Art of Loving Oneself" by Professor and former Chief Psychologist Jørn Beckmann (2011):

"It is easy to love yourself if you are emotionally independent and have taken control of your life. You abstain from claiming that others cause certain emotions in you, or that others are to blame. Instead, you claim responsibility for your emotions—and you acknowledge and accept that you are the protagonist of your own life."

In light of our review of how relational encounters lay the entire foundation of human well-being, development, and learning, it is clear that this notion of relational independence is an illusion. It is, however, an ingrained and widespread illusion, as Danish philosopher K. E. Løgstrup (1905-1981) pointed out as early as 1965:

"Nonetheless, we have this strange and unconscious notion that in the world in which a person lives his or her life, the rest of us do not properly belong. The world which to the individual is the content of his life we strangely conceive of as being that very person himself, so that the rest of us stand outside it, brushing up against it only from time to time. If, then, an encounter between humans consists only in their worlds touching briefly, only to continue unaltered in their course, none of it can mean very much at all…

In truth a very peculiar notion, no less peculiar for its obviousness to us. For the true state of affairs is quite a different one: We are each other's world and each other's destiny. There are plenty of reasons for our default manner of ignoring this." (Løgstrup 2010, 25)

And the drive towards community

Having presented the drive of human culture and nature towards easy, pleasurable solutions at the cost of the common life, it is important to underscore that even though our being has these egocentric aspects, there is among humans a common, simultaneous directedness towards forming binding relationships and communities centered around the common good. And we fortunately know that healthy, long-term relationships should not be associated with renunciation of what is pleasurable in life. People who enter into binding community and long-term relationships experience a higher degree of meaning and quality of life as well as better physical and mental health—elements with a most definite correlation to a good life of comfort and pleasure.

From the outset, humans are inherently engaged in, and powerfully drawn towards, entering into good relationships in a positive, empathic, and stimulating manner.

The ontology of empathy

In the anthology "The Relational Human" (2015, 101-102) Thor Nørretranders writes about a biological interconnectedness that constantly and inevitably binds us together:

"It is deeply ingrained in our biology that we feel each other, identify with each other, empathize and sympathize with each other: We have empathy. (…) We constantly feel each other."

By way of explaining this natural capacity for sympathy, Nørretranders points to evolutionary arguments. We are biologically endowed with empathic functions that secure our own survival and well-being. Empathy thus has an instrumental function, and one human helps the other in order to invest in his or her own well-being.

Can empathy as an instrumental phenomenon explain all charitable actions? Norwegian nurse Kari Martinsen describes how such a quantification—and biologization—of relational phenomena has serious consequences (Martinsen 1994). The approach creates a distance—in which relationships must be measured and categorized with no space and legitimacy left for emotions, intuition, and love.

According to Martinsen, human care and interplay cannot be quantified; they must be experienced as totalities. One must receive the human being in an open manner, as it finds concrete expression—and interpret the impressions and intuitions one has of the person rather than acting on—and documenting—a classification. Martinsen's phenomenological approach is especially inspired by Løgstrup, who describes such phenomena as trust, openness, and compassion as life utterances that are "given in existence" in advance. Martinsen (Overgaard 1997, 21) explains how such life utterances are spontaneously and naturally inherent in every human being, but also how we simultaneously contain other dimensions that often restrain spontaneous compassion. Therefore, one cannot count on spontaneous, intuitive compassion—one must rather learn "good conduct of life":

"The life utterances are 'born' ethical. But our moral actions demand deliberation and assessment in order for us to figure out, in each concrete situation, how best to act in accordance with the life utterance. (…) Solicitude means forming a bond. Morality becomes fundamental to the relationship. This is where power and various forms of dependence unfold through the manner in which we are emotionally present in relation to the other. There is always a keynote to any relationship. It manifests our conduct of life, and 'good conduct of life' must be learned."

As we reflect upon the nature of empathy against the background of these interpretations, we might say about empathy that it seems to be a natural part of human nature. A nature we also find reflected in the biological body. This good nature serves practical purposes, and it functions so as to bring about attachment and identification with the group.

Additionally, empathy seems to be a special property of humans, a life utterance that holds something more fundamental than mere self-optimizing instrumentalism. A spontaneous and natural human connection which cannot, however, be freely and spontaneously dissolved, and which is also challenged by the individual wish for pleasure, quality of experiences, and easy fixes. Empathy must be chosen, managed, and proportionately administered in the context of moral consideration, experience, and wisdom.

A relational psychology

In this postscript, we have described several obstacles in traditional psychology and the need for a relational and value-based psychology inspired by the anthropology of personalism. We have reviewed aspects of the human developmental process, underscoring the profoundly relational nature of human development. Furthermore, we have seen how consumer society forms a hostile environment for relationships and how humans simultaneously carry a longing for strong, sustainable relationships that encourage development.

Literature postscript

Andersen, P. & Lüchau, P (2011) Individualisering og aftraditionalisering af danskernes religiøse værdier. In: Gundelach, P. (ed.) Små og store forandringer: danskernes værdier siden 1981. Hans Reitzels Forlag.

Bech, E.M. (2014) Mig og mine følelser – en kompliceret relation. In: Bech, E.M. (ed.) Professionel kærlighed. Dafolo.

Beckmann, J. (2011) Kunsten at elske sig selv. Politikens Forlag.

Berk, L. E. (2003) Child Development. Sixth Edition. Allyn and Bacon.

Bertelsen, P. (2004) Sameksistensens grundformer – hvad kan vi lære af chimpanserne? Journal of Anthropological Psychology. No. 14, 2004.

Frello, B. (2012) Kollektiv identitet – kritiske perspektiver. Samfundslitteratur.

Gergen, K. (2006) Det mættede selv - Identitetsdilemmaer i nutiden. Dansk Psykologisk Forlag.

Haaning, A. (2003) Det indre rum i det 12. århundredes lære om sjælen. In: Filosofi og videnskabsteori på Roskilde universitetscenter, no. 3.

Harris, M & Westermann, G. (2015) A Student's guide to Developmental Psychology. Psychology Press.

Hart, S. & Møller, I. (2001) Børn, neuropsykologi og udvikling – om udviklingsforstyrrelser hos børn belyst ud fra det dynamiske samspil mellem neuropsykologiske og udviklingspsykologiske faktorer. In: Kognition & Pædagogik, no. 39, pp. 22-43.

Hart, S. & Schwartz, R. (2008) Fra interaktion til relation. Gyldendals bogklubber.

Hastrup, K. (2006). Menneske, sprog og samfund 1789-1857. In: H. Siggaard Jensen, O. Knudsen, & F. Stjernfelt (Eds.), Tankens magt: Vestens idehistorie. (Vol. 2, pp. 1304-1338). Copenhagen: Lindhardt & Ringhof.

Jacobsen, B. (2008) Læren om Sjælen. In: Pécseli, B. (ed.). Idehistorie for de pædagogiske fag. First edition. Gyldendal.

Jensen, H. (2006) Det faderløse samfund. People's Press.

Jørgensen, C. R. (2002) Find dig selv. Realiser dig selv. Konstruer dig selv. Psyke & Logos, no. 23, pp. 106-143.

Jørgensen, P.S. (2008) Identitetsdannelse i ungdomstiden. In: Brørup, M., Hauge, L. & Thomsen, U.L. (red.) Den Nye Psykologhåndbog. Gyldendal Uddannelse.

Kringelbach, M. L. (2008) Den nydelsesfulde hjerne. Gyldendal.

Løgstrup, K.E. (2010) Den etiske fordring. Klim.

Martinsen, K. (1994) Fra Marx til Løgstrup, Om etik og sanselighed i sygeplejen. Munksgaard.

Nielsen, K. & Tanggaard, L. (2011) Pædagogisk psykologi – en grundbog. Samfundslitteratur.

Nordisk ministerråd (2001) Forbrugernes fornemmelse for etik. TemaNord 2001:583.

Nørretranders, T. (2015) Vær nær – Sammenhæng i sammenfundet. Chapter in: Lumholdt, K. & Norgaard Mortensen, J. (ed.) Det relationelle menneske. Vindelsti.

Overgaard, A.E. (1997) Kari Martinsen: Sanselig sygepleje. Sygeplejersken 1997; (7): pp. 18-22.

Pine, B. J. & Gilmore, J. H. (1999): The Experience Economy. Harvard Business School Press.

Richter, L. (2011) Ensomhed har konsekvenser for alle. Information 11-16-2016.

Rose, Nikolas (1998): Inventing our selves. Cambridge University Press.

Sprogøe, J. (2008) Pædagogik. In: Pécseli, B. (ed). Idehistorie for de pædagogiske fag. First edition. Gyldendal.

Waldinger, R. (2016) What makes a good life? Lessons from the longest study on happiness. https://www.youtube.com/watch?v=8KkKuTCFvzI

Ugilt, R. (2015) Nydelse. Aarhus Universitetsforlag.

Zupancic, Alenka (2008). The Odd One In. Cambridge MA.

Notes

1) Australian Nurse Bronnie Ware has written a book about what dying people regret the most. Number two on the list is the regret of having worked too hard. Bronnie Ware: *The Top Five Regrets of the Dying* (Hay House, 2012).

2) N. F. S. Grundtvig's song "Langt højere bjerge så vide på jord" from 1820.

3) In philosophical and academic terms, the matter may be put as follows: Personalism is an anthropology that poses the *person* as ethical, ontological, and epistemological primate, as the point of departure for existence and the privileged aspect of being as well as the foundation for all knowledge. That is to say, what is good (ethics), what is (ontology), and how to understand it all (epistemology) must start from the person as first principle.

4) Anthony Giddens sought a third way that would escape the dichotomy of socialism vs. capitalism. His endeavor took the form of a so-called Social-Democratic philosophy in which Giddens claimed that the global political situation had outgrown the socialist demand for the abolition of capitalism and that the ethical demands of socialism might be met within a capitalist market-based system, namely through efforts of the state to provide equal *opportunities* within the capitalist system.
In an attempt to renew itself under the leadership of Tony Blair and Gordon Brown, the British Labour Party drew upon Giddens' philosophy, distancing itself from the trade unions, vocally endorsing free market economics, and shifting its ethical focus from social equality to "social justice."

5) Martin Buber unfolds these thoughts in his most famous book: *I and Thou* (Scribner, 2000).

6) J. B. L. Knox: *Gabriel Marcel : håbets filosof, fortvivlelsens dramatiker* (Syddansk Universitetsforlag, 2003).

7) Gabriel Marcel: *Homo Viator: Introduction to a Metaphysic of Hope* (Harper Torchbooks, 1962), p. 60; J. B. L. Knox: *Gabriel Marcel. Håbets filosof, fortvivlelsens dramatiker* (Syddansk Universitetsforlag, 2003), p. 119.

8) Gabriel Marcel: *Homo Viator: Introduction to a Metaphysic of Hope* (Harper Torchbooks, 1962); *The Mystery of Being* (The Harvill Press, 1951).

9) Emmanuel Mounier: *Personalism* (The Grove Press, 1952), p. 20.

10) Karol Wojtyla unfolds these ideas in *The Acting Person* (D. Reidel Publishing Company, 1979) and *Person and Community. Selected Essays* (Peter Lang, 1993). The quote is from Pope John Paul II's *Letter to Families*, 1994, see www.vatican.va.

11) Karol Wojtyla: *Veritatis Splendor* – Papal encyclical letter (Libreria Editrice Vaticana, 1993 – www.vatican.va), paragraph 49, with reference to the constitutional or confessional document *Gaudium et Spes* (Joy and hope) from the Second Vatican Council of 1962-1965.

12) See Juan Manuel Burgos: *El Personalismo* (Ediciones Palabra, 2000); *Introducción al Personalismo* (Ediciones Palabra, 2012); *Antropología* (Palabra, 2003).

13) Karol Wojtyla: *Uczestnictwo czy alienacja.* (Participation or Alienation). Paper at the Fourth International Phenomenology Conference on January 24-28, 1975 in Fribourg, Switzerland. English translation published as "Participation or Alienation" in *Person and Community. Selected Essays* (Peter Lang, 1993), pp. 197-207.

14) Bronnie Ware: *The Top Five Regrets of the Dying* (Hay House, 2012).

15) Peter Rollins: *Insurrection* (Howard Books, 2011), p. 2-3.

16) Quoted from debate on Danish public radio.

17) John T. Cacioppo interviewed in Danish newspaper *Information*: "Ensomhed har konsekvenser for alle," on November 15, 2011. The study showing that loneliness is as dangerous as smoking fifteen cigarettes per day was carried out at Brigham Young University in the U.S. and published as "Social Relationships and Mortality Risk" in the journal *PLoS Medicin* in 2010.

18) www.oecdbetterlifeindex.org.

19) *The Telegraph* on September 14, 2009. Read more about Joseph E. Stiglitz's work at www.stiglitzsenfitoussi.fr.

20) *Journal of Gerontology: Social Sciences*: "From Social Structural Factors to Perceptions of Relationship Quality and Loneliness," 2008, Vol. 63B, No. 6, pp. 375–384.

21) Quoted from Danish public radio. For further reference see www.kringelbach.dk.

22) Christopher Lasch: *The Culture of Narcissism* (W. W. Norton & Company, 1979).

23) Danish Newspaper *Weekendavisen* on September 21, 2012.

24) Sherry Turkle: *Alone together: why we expect more from technology and less from each other* (Basic Books, 2011).

25) Sheldon, Abad and Hinsch: "A twoprocess view of Facebook use and relatedness needsatisfaction: Disconnection drives use, and connection rewards it" in *Journal of Personality and Social Psychology*, January 2011.

26) Sources: Health and Safety Executive, Labour Force Survey, Safe Work Australia, European Agency for Safety and Health at Work, The Work Foundation, Health Advocate, World Health Organization.

27) Ove K. Pedersen: *Konkurrencestaten* (Hans Reitzel, 2011), from chapter 6: "Skolen og den opportunistiske person," pp. 169-203.

28) Ove K. Pedersen: *Konkurrencestaten* (Hans Reitzel, 2011), from chapter 6: "Skolen og den opportunistiske person," pp. 169-203.

29) Ove K. Pedersen: *Konkurrencestaten* (Hans Reitzel, 2011), from chapter 6: "Skolen og den opportunistiske person," pp. 169-203.

30) Quoted from Danish public radio.

31) Victim-offender conference coordinator Charlotte Wegener in Danish newspaper *Politiken* on January 9, 2011.

32) See for instance www.restorativejustice.org.

33) Desmond Tutu: *No Future Without forgiveness* (Doubleday 1999), p. 31.

34) Desmond Tutu: *No Future Without forgiveness* (Doubleday 1999), p. 35. For further reference see Michael Battle: *Ubuntu I in You, and You in Me* (Seabury Books, 2009) with a preface by Desmond Tutu, and Desmond Tutu: *God Is Not a Christian* (HarperOne 2011), pp. 21-24.

35) Desmond Tutu: *God Is Not a Christian* (HarperOne 2011), p. 22.

36) JeanPaul Sartre: *No Exit* (Vintage International, 1989). The famous dictum is found in Sartre's stage play *No Exit* from 1944.

37) Emmanuel Mounier: *Personalism* (The Grove Press, 1952), p. 18.

38) Emmanuel Mounier: *Personalism* (The Grove Press, 1952), p. 18.

39) Emmanuel Mounier: *Personalism* (The Grove Press, 1952), p. 58.

40) Emmanuel Mounier: *Personalism* (The Grove Press, 1952), p. 64.

41) Emmanuel Mounier: *Manifeste au Service du Personalisme* (available online at classiques.uqac.ca), part 4, ch. 2.

42) See John Paul II's encyclical letter *Centesimus Annus* (Libreria Editrice Vaticana, 1991 – www.vatican.va).

43) See Tobias J. Lanz (ed.): *Beyond Capitalism & Socialism* (Light in the Darkness Publications, 2008).

44) N. F. S. Grundtvig in the journal *Danskeren* 1949, p. 540.

45) Hal Koch: "D.U.s fremtid," *Lederbladet* no. 6, 1945.

46) Hal Koch: "D.U.s fremtid," *Lederbladet* no. 6, 1945.

47) Howard Kurtz: *Spin Cycle: Inside the Clinton Propaganda Machine* (Pan Books, 1998).

48) Hal Koch: *Hvad er demokrati?* (Gyldendal, 1995), p. 16.

49) Alexis de Tocqueville, *Democracy in America* (The Floating Press, 2009) p. 234.

50) Richard Stengel "A Time to Serve" in *Time* on July 30, 2007.

51) Robert D. Putnam: *Making Democracy Work. Civic Traditions in Modern Italy* (Princeton University Press, 1993); "The Prosperous Community. Social Capital and Public Life" (*The American Prospect*, 1993, no. 13, pp. 35-42); "Bowling Alone: America's Declining Social Capital" (*Journal of Democracy*, 1995, vol. 5, no. 1, pp. 65-78).

52) Thomas O Buford, *Trust, Our Second Nature: Crisis, Reconciliation and the Personal* (Lexington Books, 2009) p. 3.

53) Hal Koch: *Hvad er demokrati?* (Gyldendal, 1995), p. 13.

54) Sources: Corporation for National and Community Service, World Volunteer Web.

55) European Parliament: *The role of volunteering in contributing to economic and social cohesion* (Case number 2007/2149(INI), passed on April 22, 2008).

56) United Nations and Johns Hopkins University: *Measuring Civil Society and Volunteering: Initial Findings from Implementation of the UN Handbook on Nonprofit Institutions*, 2007 and *Handbook on Non-Profit Institutions in the System of National Accounts*, 2003. See www.jhu.edu/ccss.

57) Robert Putnam has carried out extensive research concerning social capital. See for instance *Making Democracy Work. Civic Traditions in Modern Italy* (Princeton University Press, 1993) and "The Prosperous Community. Social Capital and Public Life," in *The American Prospect*, 1993, no 13, pp. 35-42.

58) Sartre was strongly inspired by German existential philosopher Martin Heidegger, not least concerning the notion of "thrownness into the world." See Martin Heidegger: *Being and Time* (Harper & Row, 2008).

59) Strictly speaking, we are dealing here with what Sartre termed "atheistic existentialism." Theistic and Christian existentialism arguably have more in common with personalism.

60) Karol Wojtyla: *Uczestnictwo czy alienacja* (Participation or Alienation). Paper at the Fourth International Phenomenology Conference on January 24-28, 1975 in Fribourg, Switzerland. English translation published as "Participation or Alienation" in *Person and Community. Selected Essays* (Peter Lang, 1993), pp. 197-207.

61) Emmanuel Mounier: *The spoil of the violent* (Cross Currents, 1955). Translated from *L'affrontement Chretien*.

62) Emmanuel Levinas: *Totality and Infinity* (Kluwer Academic Publishers, 1991).

63) Emmanuel Levinas: *Difficult Freedom* (Johns Hopkins University Press, 1990), p. 291.

64) Immanuel Kant: *Grounding for the Metaphysics of Morals* (Cambridge University Press, 1998), p. 42.

65) Christian Smith: *What is a person? Rethinking Humanity, Social Life, and Moral Good from the Person Up* (The University of Chicago Press, 2010).

66) Nikolai Berdyaev: *End of Our Time* (Sheed and Ward, 1933); *Slavery and Freedom* (C. Scribner's Sons, 1944); *The Destiny of Man* (The Centenary Press, 1945); *Dream and Reality* (Geoffrey Bles, 1950).

67) The Bible: *The Gospel According to Luke* chapter 6, verse 31. Immanuel Kant: *Grounding for the Metaphysics of Morals* (Hackett, 1993), p. 30

68) Recent years have seen the use of the concept *personism* to refer the notion that a human does not really acquire value or dignity until having become a rational and conscious person. This new use of the concept of personhood is fundamentally opposed to classical personalism, which would attack any idea of reducing human worth to rationality and consciousness. The new use of the concept of personhood may be attributed in particular to Australian moral philosopher Peter Singer (1946-), who precisely ties dignity and ethical obligation towards others to personality and rationality. It would be lamentable for the new concept of "personism" to be confused with personalism since it not only goes against the classical personalist tradition, but also creates conceptual confusion and diminishes the value of both concepts. In the anthology *Ethical Personalism*, Josef Seifert deals with this problematic, calling Peter Singer distinctly anti-personalist. See Josef Seifert: "Personalism and Personalisms" in Cheikh Gueye: *Ethical Personalism* (Ontos Verlag, 2011).

69) See Thomas D. Williams: *Who Is My Neighbor: Personalism and the*

Foundations of Human Rights. (The Catholic University of America Press, 2005).

70) K. E. Løgstrup: *Den etiske fordring* (Gyldendal 1956), pp. 25-26.

71) Claudio Magris in Italian newspaper *Corriere della Sera*, quoted in Danish Newspaper *Information* on June 6, 2011.

72) Karl Ove Knausgård "Mit fædreland" published in Danish weekly paper *Weekendavisen* on August 19, 2011; Danish paper *Information* on August 18, 2011. German-Jewish philosopher Hannah Arendt (1906-1975) calls this "the banality of evil" and warns us that both totalitarian systems and modern mass culture pose a threat to freedom and human dignity. According to Arendt, freedom is coterminous with action, and community is the necessary condition for such freedom. However, due to the dissolution of civil society in modern societies, humans have become atomized, anonymous individuals within great and powerful systems. See Hannah Arendt: *The Human Condition* (University of Chicago Press, 1958) and *The Origins of Totalitarianism* (Schocken Books, 1951).

73) Nikolai Berdyaev: *Slavery and Freedom* (C. Scribner's Sons, 1944).

74) Nicolas Berdyaev: *The Russian Idea* (The Macmillan Company, 1948) p. 243.

75) Václav Havel: *Disturbing the Peace* (Faber and Faber, 1990), p. 11.

76) Václav Havel: *Politics and Conscience,* section IV (available online at www.vaclavhavel.cz).

77) Luk Bouckaert: "Introduction: personalism" in *Ethical Perspectives*, April 1999.

78) Václav Havel: *Summer Meditations* (Vintage, 1993) and "The Power of the Powerless" in Václav Havel et al.: *The Power of the Powerless* (Routledge, 2009).

79) Emmanuel Mounier: *A Personalist Manifesto.* Translated from the French by the monks of St. John's Abbey, Collegeville, Minnesota (Longmans, Green and Co., 1938).

80) Max Scheler: *Der Formalismus in der Ethik und die Materiale Wertethik:*

Neuer Versuch der Grundlegung eines Ethischen Personalismus (Gesammelte Werke, vol. 2. Francke Verlag, 1980); *Politisch Pädago- gische Schriften* (Gesammelte Werke, vol. 4. Francke Verlag, 1982); Stephen Frederick Schneck: *Person and polis: Max Scheler's personalism as political theory* (State University of New York Press, 1987).

81) Mary Keys: *Aquinas, Aristotle, and the Promise of the Common Good* (Cambridge University Press, 2006).

82) Martin Luther King: *Letter From Birmingham Jail*, April 16, 1963.

83) Martin Luther King: "A Comparison of the Conceptions of God in the Thinking of Paul Tillich and Henry Nelson Wieman", 15 April 1955, in *The Papers of Martin Luther King vol. II – Rediscovering Precious Values* (University of California Press, 1994) pp. 339-544.

84) Martin Luther King: "The Personalism of J. M. E. McTaggert under Criticism," published in Clayborne Carson: *The Papers of Martin Luther King, Jr.* (University of California Press Carson, 1994) vol. 2, pp. 61-76.

85) Martin Luther King: *Stride toward Freedom* (Harper & Row, 1958), p. 100.

86) Borden Parker Bowne: *Personalism* (Mifflin and Company, 1908).

87) Edgar S. Brightman: *Is God a Person?* (Association Press, 1932), p. 4.

88) Edgar S. Brightman: "Personalism (Including Personal Idealism)" in *A History of Philosophical Systems*, ed. Vergilius Ferm (The Philosophical Library, 1950).

89) See Albert C. Knudson: *The Philosophy of Personalism. A Study in the Metaphysics of Religion* (The Abingdon Press, 1927).

90) Erica Chenoweth and Maria J. Stephan: *Why Civilian Resistance Works* (Columbia University Press, 2011).

91) A 2011 survey by the Pew Research Center, quoted by IPS News on September 1, 2011, shows that the number of U.S. citizens who deemed torture acceptable rose from a minority of 43 percent in 2004 to a majority of 53 percent in 2011. Simultaneously, the population segment who found that torture could never be acceptable fell from 32 to 24 percent.

92) Emmanuel Mounier: *Personalism* (The Grove Press, 1952), p. viii.

93) Emmanuel Mounier: "Personalismen," article in Danish journal *Heretica*, 1950, vol. 3, pp. 182-201.

94) Uffe Østergård: Speech given at a diocese council meeting, Conference Center Trinity, Fredericia, Denmark, September 23, 2005.

95) Herman Van Rompuy: "Du personnalisme à l'action politique," speech given at Grandes Conférences Catholiques Bruxelles, December 7, 2009.

96) Denis de Rougemont quoted in Jacques Delors: "Personalist Reflections" in *Ethical Perspectives* vol. 6 (1999), no. 1, p. 82.

97) Jacques Delors: "Personalist Reflections" in *Ethical Perspectives* vol. 6 (1999), no. 1, p. 82. Delors' entire speech from September 30, 1999 is available online in French at www.coleurope.eu.

98) Rufus Burrow: *Personalism. A Critical Introduction* (Chalice Press, 1999).

99) Rune Lykkeberg: "Det frie valgs lidelser," column in *Information*, November 26, 2011.

100) See Barry Schwartz: *The Paradox of Choice: Why More is Less* (Ecco, 2004).

101) Lise Andersen: "Hvad er det, vi jagter? Velfærd eller velstand?" in Danish newspaper *Berlingske Tidende*, November 12, 2011.

102) Nikolai Berdyaev: *Slavery and Freedom* (C. Scribner's Sons, 1944).

103) Emilia van Hauen: *Farvel egofest* (Akademisk, 2009), pp. 216-217.

104) Knud Aarup: *Frivillighedens velfærdssamfund* (Frydenlund, 2010), p. 210.

105) Serge Latouche: "Degrowth Economics" in *Le Monde Diplomatique*, November, 2004.

Index

A

Aarup, Knud, 123
abstract, 90-
actions, 76
active citizenship, 67-
Adenuaer, Konrad, 113, 115
affrontement, 78
alienation, 37, 75, 100
Andersen, Lise, 121
animals, 85
anthropology, 20-
anti-political politic, 95-
apartheid, 52
Aquinas, St. Thomas, 86, 101
Aristotle, 100, 126
authenticity, 136

B

Bakunin, Mikail, 58
Bauman, Zygmunt, 136
Beckmann, Jørgen, 145
Belloc, Hilaire, 60
Berdyaev, Nikolai, 85, 92-, 121-
Berdyaev's Sundays, 95

Bergson, Henri, 98
Better Life Index, OECD, 40
biololization, 147
Bjørnskov, Christian, 40
Boethius, 127
Boston personalism, 104-
Bowne, Borden Parker, 104
brain, 138
Brightman, Edgar S., 105
Brunschvicg, Léon, 82
Buber, Martin, 30-, 102
Buford, Thomas O., 70
bureaucracy, 92-
Burgos, Juan Manuel, 37
brain, 42

C

Cacioppo, John T., 41
Campbell, Keith, 44
capitalism, 98-
Catholic Church, 36
centralization, 92-
civil rights, 100-
Charta 77, 96

Chenoweth, Erica, 106
Chesterton, G. K., 60
choices, 76
collectivism, 19-, 30, 116-
commercialization, 121-
common good, the, 101
community, 64, 146
competition State, 46-
concrete, 90-
connectedness, 90
consumption, 121-, 143
control, 69-
conversation, 64-
counteraction, 123-

D

Darwinian philosophy, 105
de-growth movement, 124
de Gasperi, Alcide, 113, 115
de Rougemont, Denis, 114
de Tocqueville, Alexis, 66
decisions, 75
Delors, Jacques, 115
democracy, 62-
depression, 140
Descartes, René, 36
dehumanized, 51-, 104
depersonalization, 26, 54, 118
dialogical personalism, 82
dialogue, 64-
dignity, 81-, 87-, 107-, 114
distributists, 60
Dostoyevsky, Fyodor, 95

E

economy, 98-
economic liberalism, 61
emotionalization, 136
empathy, 147
engaged, 57-
engagement, 57-, 67
entropy, 93, 120-
equality, 87-
Esprit, 58, 112
ethical, 147-
EU, 70, 114-
existential answers, 133
existentialism, 75
Europe, 65
extended families, 48

F

family, 48
Fatherless Society, The, 134
Fathers of Europe, 113-
folk high school (folkehøjskole), 63
freedom, 57-, 87-

G

Gandhi, Mahatma, 102, 106
GDP – Gross Domestic Product, 40
Giddens, Anthony, 26
Gilson, Etienne, 95
greatness, 75
Grundtvig, N.F.S., 60-

H

Hamlet, Price, 64
happiness, 40
Havel, Václav, 95-
Hegel, G. W. F., 94
Heidegger, Martin, 82
Herbart, J. F., 132
Hitler, Adolf, 30
Holocaust, 92
humanism, 85-
Husserl, Edmund, 82, 98
Huxley, Aldous, 92

I

identity, 140
illusion, 145
independency, 145
individualism, 34-, 116-, 130-
indoctrination, 121-
integrated humanism, 86
interdependency, 90

J

Jensen, Henrik, 134
Jesus, 89
Jørgensen, Carsten René, 136

K

Kant, Emmanuel, 84, 89, 94, 98
Kringelbach, Morten L., 42
Kahlo, Frida, 42

Kierkegaard, Søren, 95
King, Martin Luther, 100-
Knausgård, Karl Ove, 91
Knudson, Albert C., 105
Koch, Hal, 62-
Kurtz, Howard, 65
Piaget, Jean, 131

L

Lasch, Christopher, 42
legal system, 49
Levinas, Emmanuel, 81-
Lindgren, Astrid, 29
loneliness, 140
Lossky, N.O., 95
Lykkeberg, Rune, 121
Løgstrup, K. E., 46, 90, 93, 145

M

Macintyre, Alasdair, 134
Marcel, Gabriel, 32-, 95
Magris, Claudio, 91
Maritain, Jacques, 86-
Martinsen, Kari, 147
Marxism, 100-
materialism, 85
Metheny, Rachel, 118
Monnet, Jean, 115
morality, 147
Mounier, Emmanuel, 34, 57-, 74, 111-
multicultural society, 54

N

narcissism, 42
natural law, 100-
nature, 85
neurons, 139
New Labour, British, 26
Nietzsche, Friedrich, 95, 98
nonviolent resistance, 103-
Nørretranders, Thor, 147

O

objectification, 93
Occupy Wall Street, 67
OECD, 40
oikos, 48
openness, 147

P

pacifism, 107
Parks, Rosa, 102
participation, 38, 75
Pascal, Blaise, 99
Patočka, Jan, 97
Pedersen, Ove Kaj, 46
person, 81-
personal, 90-
Philosopher's Ship, 95
pleasure, 142
politicization, 63, 66
politics, 58
postmodern, 136
power, 118

Pope John Paul II, 36-
Prague personalist, 97
price, 84
psychology, 129-
psychologization, 135
Putnam, Robert, 68

R

reconciliation, 50-
relational, 29-, 137-
relational psychology, 136-, 148
relationships, 57, 83, 141
resistance, 103-
responsibility, 74-, 95-, 122
restorative justice, 50
rights, 87-
Rivera, Diego, 42
Rollins, Peter, 39
Rose, Nikolas, 131
Roman law, 126-

S

Sartre, Jean-Paul, 25, 42, 57, 74
Scandinavian model, 19
Scheler, Max, 95, 98-
Schleiermacher, Friedrich,
Schopenhauer, Arthur, 94
Schumann, Robert, 113, 115
Sedaka, Niel, 76
self-development, 133-
self-optimization, 133-
self-realization, 133-
Shakespeare, William, 64

Sharp, Gene, 106
Smith, Adam, 19
Smith, Christian, 84
social capital, 68-
social cohesion, 54
Solitaire, 76
Spencer, Herbert, 105
spin, 64-
spirit, 85-
Stengel, Richard, 68
Stephan, Maria J., 106
Stiglitz, Joseph, 40
Stoltenberg, Jens, 91
stress, 44
systems, 92-
systemic failure, 46-, 92-, 120-

T

Tertullian, 126
the common good, 60-
Theoderix, king, 127
Tillich, Paul, 102
TimeBank, 72
Tolstoy, Lev, 95
totalitarianism, 116
transvalutation, 93
trust, 69-
Truth and Reconliation Committee, 52
Turkle, Sherry, 45
Tutu, Desmond, 51-, 103-
Twenge, Jean, 44

U

ubuntu, 52
UN, 87-, 118-
UN Human Rights Declaration, 87-, 107

V

value, 84, 88, 131-
Van Hauen, Emilia, 119, 123
Van Rompuy, Herman, 114
voluntary activities, 70-
volunteering, 72

W

Wahl, Jean, 82
Waldinger, Robert, 137
Warhol, Andy, 43
Weber, Max, 99
Wegener, Charlotte, 49
Wieman, Henry Nelson, 102
Williams, Thomas D., 89
Winnicot, Donald W., 131
welfare state, 46
World Health Organization, WHO, 45
Wojtyla, Karol, 36-, 75

Z

Zupančič, Alenka, 144

Ø

Østergaard, Uffe, 114-

About the Author

Jonas Norgaard Mortensen has been a key figure in an effort to interpret and communicate personalism in a Danish and Nordic culture. He has published Det fælles bedste. Introduktion til personalismen (2012), The Common Good. An Introduction to Personalism (2014) and the two anthologies Det personlige samfund. Personalisme i praksis (in English: The Personal Society. Personalism in practice) (2015) and Det relationelle menneske. Personalisme i perspektiv (in English: The Relational Human. Personalism in Perspective) (2015) in which 48 prominent leaders in the Danish society unfolds personalism within their different fields of knowledge and work.

In 2017 Jonas Norgaard Mortensen has published Personalismens idéhistorie. En akademisk undersøgelse (in English: Personalism's history of ideas. An academic study) and has been the editor of the book Tanke og Handling skal være eet. Personalismen i Frankrig (in English: Thought and action should be one. Personalism in France) by the danish theologian and philosopher K.E. Løgstrup.

Photographer: *Søren Kjeldgaard*

Jonas Norgaard Mortensen is today an active lecturer, working both nationally and internationally with personalism and is director of the Institute for Relational Psychology, working with relations key role in education, welfare, leadership and society. The Institute will in 2017 publish a book that examines and reflects on how personalism may constitute an anthropological and value orientation foundation of psychology.

Jonas Norgaard Mortensen was born in 1976; he holds degrees in political science, literature, and leadership; he is married to Hanne Skovgaard and father to Johan, Selma and Oline.

www.ingramcontent.com/pod-product-compliance
Lightning Source LLC
Chambersburg PA
CBHW061839300426
44115CB00013B/2445